Digital Engineering:
Complex System Design

S. Mathioudakis

authorHOUSE

AuthorHouse™ UK
1663 Liberty Drive
Bloomington, IN 47403 USA
www.authorhouse.co.uk
Phone: UK TFN: 0800 0148641 (Toll Free inside the UK)
        UK Local: (02) 0369 56322 (+44 20 3695 6322 from outside the UK)

Published by AuthorHouse 07/27/2024

ISBN: 979-8-8230-8871-8 (sc)
ISBN: 979-8-8230-8879-4 (e)

Library of Congress Control Number: 2024914721

Print information available on the last page.

Contents

Foreword

This text book offers the reader an overview into creating a computer from an electrical design perspective. Throughout the book are a number of diagrams explaining how a computer would be designed as a circuit. The expectation of the author is to simplify the process of designing computers by explaining how it would be possible to implement a simple process. The book itself looks at a 16 bit computer with a few sets of instructions. Detailing the processes involved in design.

This is the second text book of three which aim to explore computer science. The author hopes to finish the compendium with a book on software engineering, which explores the paradigms needed to create successful programs and programming structures.

Preface

The purpose of this textbook is to outline and explore some of the assumptions and structures, which underpin the design of digital systems. The intention is that the reader is then able to create their own processes and design their own digital circuits. The book achieves these aims in a number of ways, the system inside a computer is broken down into a number of structures, such as I/O communication and CPU design. Hopefully explaining how these parts work and what tasks they carry out during a programme or performing complex procedures. The book is split into a number of parts which look at digital logic design, creating the structures within components and finally deals with the subject of designing small systems. Each part tries to investigate how a computer might work at a basic level and describes other structures needed in larger computers like todays 64 bit machines.

Throughout the text computer architecture is explained in a high level of detail, analysing designs and communicating how to create certain processes. The schematics formatted for the book describe the processes at the basis of transistor logic and the interfacing of components and data transfers. Although it is necessary to point out, that this is mainly to allow the reader to understand the process without being completely accurate. Most of the circuits explained here would actually work, but larger systems have moved on in such a way that older structures which the 16 bit machines used are no-longer necessary As this textbook mainly focuses on 16 bit machine processes, it may limit the reader in terms of their approach to the complex programming of todays sophisticated computers.

The intention is that the information found within the writings should bring to light the basic design and structure of a computer system. Although the overall design appears less complicated than some computer processes. The design of a basic system should be able to be achieved. The approaches found here should provide enough insight to actually build a working computerised system.

Part 1

Combinational Systems and Procedures

Combinational Digital Circuits

In this chapter you will look at the following

- Logic gates
- Truth tables and Kernaugh maps
- Latches
- Combinational logic systems

1.1.1 What does combinational logic refer to?

This is a term which describes a part of the process which computers use to infer meaningful data from simple logic structures. Computers tend to think by inputting a simple value as a binary 1 or 0 and re-determining this value or logic state as a new entity or definition. For example when computers analyse data the information may be presented as '0010 0110' This will then be interpreted by a decoder and translated by the computer as a logic sequence or number etc, in binary this data could have a number of different representations depending on where the code was being used. Combinational logic describes some of the processes which are used to manipulate this data set. Essentially the combinational circuit or logic, will create the pathways or gates which allow the binary to be translated. These systems are used a lot inside computers as data is constantly being moved around the system, modified and processed.

Not all systems use combinational logic for example some outputs such as audio and analogue systems, have no need to use logic states or digital sequences, as the information which the signal is trying to send does not need to use this form of translation. By the term digital logic system we mean anything which revaluates code and provides meaningful data from this analysis. For example a small computer may use a number of LCD segment displays to present the result of the calculation of two numbers. Combinational logic could be used here in a number of ways. The segment display would need a decoder to decode the binary and present the correct figure on the LCD. There would also be a number system in place which tells the computer what the value is from the initial binary code.

For instance

0110 = 6 in decimal
1010 = 10 in decimal

Or

0100 = 4 on a segment display
0111 = 7 on a segment display

This basic form of binary shows that one system is interpreted by the computer as a different value. Meaning the data has it own value set and needs to be interpreted by the computers structure. Combinational logic provides a method of completing this calculus. Bringing about meaningful data through the manipulation of code. The above example had two uses for logic systems. Computers have many more of these types of processes which are completed in a number of ways throughout a simple program or routine. A principle of computer logic or combinational systems is creating methods of reducing complex structures into smaller numbers of gates or pathways. A computer designer ideally should create the process to use the simplest form or least number of pathways. Later in the chapter K maps will be used to reduce a problem involving digital pathways. This kind of technique is useful when designing encoders or instruction sets.

1.2.1 Simple logic circuits

The simplest circuits within combination logic are made out of logic gates. These can be used when a value is determined from a number of inputs. For example a logic gate would act like a switch which turns an outputted value to 1 or 'on' depending on the state of two inputs. In this instance we might use an AND gate which has two inputs and one output. If both inputs receive a signal there would be a return value output. A relay system might have a safety switch would act in a similar way, where it relies on both inputs to work. In fact within digital logic there are various forms of logic gates which work in different ways to reinterpret the value of a number of inputs. Logic gates are also not constrained by the number of inputs. The figure below shows the picture typically designated for each type of gate.

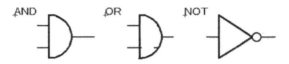

Fig: 1.2.1 three logic gates (AND, OR, NOT)

   As mentioned, each gate works slightly differently due to the mapping of the circuits inside the gate. For instance an OR gate will work if either input has a voltage source. Whereas the AND gate needs both voltages or the output would not be able to produce a signal. Due to the characteristics of each type of gate it is possible to create digital circuits with have a number of possible uses. Simple digital circuits are used to decode information. More complex types are used for decoding video and audio information. This is where a simple signal needs to be transformed into a better-quality digital output. The logic gates are used to re-evaluate a source signal by decoding the information. To explain how a logic gate works it is necessary to plot the expected output of a system against a truth table. Which states the logic input and the expected decoded output. Truth tables are not only useful within logic gates and are also used to solve larger processes. For instance it might be necessary to visualise an entire system, by creating a truth table which explores the expected output for each logic state.

AND GATE		
A	**B**	**Out**
1	0	0
0	1	0
0	0	0
1	1	1

OR GATE		
A	**B**	**Out**
1	0	1
0	1	1
0	0	0
1	1	1

NOT GATE		
A	**B**	**Out**
1	0	0
0	1	0
0	0	1
1	1	0

Fig: 1.2.1 Truth tables (AND, OR, NOT)

1.2.2 Using transistors as logic gates

Truth tables and logic gates are used to visually describe the process of simple systems. They are a graphical tool for exploring how they might appear on a circuit, or for evaluating the usages within a digital system. From a design perspective this is useful as it is possible to describe the process of a circuit. However from an electronic and engineering perspective, the logic gates, are seen as the application of small transistors connected inside a circuit. To develop this idea further the figure below describes a number of gates which create the same state as the truth table. Except here a voltage source needs to be applied for the circuit to work. The output will depend on the design of the logic gate. The design of these circuits can be easily created using transistors. This knowledge is essential for the careful design of digital systems, where circuits are able to be created from the connection of a few transistors. In fact integrated chips currently use this in the construction of logic states in IC chips.

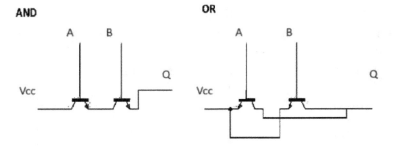

Fig: 1.2.2 Transistor logic gates

1.3.1 Abstraction of logic circuits

Combinational logic can be represented in truth tables or through using other tools such as Kernaugh maps. Here a logic system can be designed by describing how the system is intended to work. For example binary code might need to be represented in a decimal format, or a MUX needs to create a binary sequence from the application of two processes being carried out at the same time. These types of examples could use a truth table to translate how the code might be presented to the signal source. Here the expected output could be predicted by the information presented to the inputs. If we look at the diagram below the digital logic here has three inputs A, B and C. while only having one output. This is represented within programming as the value 'F' or output.

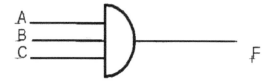

Fig: 1.3.1 Digital logic first sequence

In terms of abstraction of the data we can present the information as:

ABC = F

This reflects the state 'F' being on if Conditions in inputs ABC are all on. If we have another value.

A$\underline{BC}$ = F

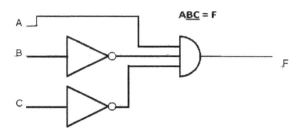

Fig: 1.3.1 Digital logic second sequence

Here the problem has slightly changed as now for the value F to create a signal source; A needs to be connected, whereas BC will be 0 or contain no connection to source.

1.3.2 Why use abstractions?

Abstraction is used within computer hardware and also within in the design of processor's software. The principle here is that a computer could be designed within a number of ways and provide the same expected output as a number of different systems. Whereas due to the extended complexity of computers, it is necessary to simplify the circuitry inside the computer chassis. This makes it not only easier to build but simplifies some of the terms used within the design of the software. Abstraction provides one simple process of describing the circuit and building a less complicated version which provides the same expectation of outputs.

1.3.3 An example of redesigning a small circuit

Here I will explain another scenario where it is possible to redesign a circuit using a Kernaugh map. Here the circuit has three inputs and one output. Unlike the other circuit, the output F will have a signal source at the output under two conditions. This can be represented in the following format.

$F = A\underline{B}C.\underline{AB}C$

The problem can be also be developed using a truth table, which describes the value obtained for the result of the digital logic sequence from the inputs. The truth table describes each state which the three inputs can produce.

Truth Table

A	B	C	Out
1	0	0	0
0	1	0	0
0	0	1	1
1	1	0	0
1	1	1	0
0	1	1	0
1	0	1	1
0	0	0	0

Fig: 1.3.3 Truth table of combinational logic problem

Through looking at the truth table and the abstraction it is possible to observe that the output has a constant value for C. Which means it is possible to alter the truth table into a Kernaugh map which takes the value C out of the equation and is plotted against the various sequences of AB. Plotting these values provides a much smaller truth table. Making it easier to design the expected outputs. The K map plotted below describes the system by limiting certain values to a denominator.

K Map

AB	C	Output
00	1	1
01	1	0
10	1	1
11	1	0

Fig 1.3.3 Kernaugh map plot of expected outputs

Here we can see that by limiting the values of the formula it is easier to create a smaller abstraction of terms to use within the truth table. Below is the formula seen as a sequence of logical gates, which has been designed from the expected outputs. The output presented by F will be identical to the results found in the truth table. Sometimes within creating or designing a sequence of logic gates, it is possible to rewire the system once the value F has been determined. Meaning that it might be possible to redesign how the gates are connected.

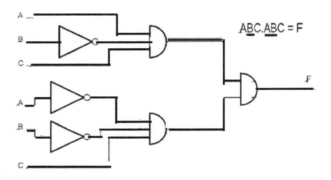

Fig: 1.3.3 Logical representation of F = A$\overline{BC}$.A$\overline{BC}$

1.4.1 Understanding latches and storing binary

What has been explained so far is the use of digital logic, its design and evaluation using abstraction. This is a very useful technique when designing certain parts of digital systems, as the system needs to be carefully designed so that the circuit works without errors during computational processes. Digital circuits can also be created using other forms of digital networks. For instance digital logic can be developed into complex sequences to obtain circuits which perform a high number of calculations. Other types of circuits need a form of memory so data can be stored and processed. This means that the circuitry inside the computer has to be able to retain a small amount of information presented in a form of binary format. This can be achieved through the use of logic gates connected in special types of sequences. For instance, SR latch can be designed within a circuit using two OR gates in sequence. If a clock is added to this same circuit, it becomes a D Flip Flop, which is used within the storing of binary data.

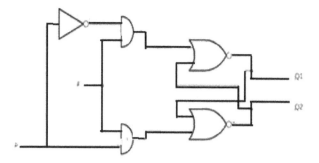

Fig: 1.4.1 D Flip Flop designed from logic gates

The diagram above describes how a number of logic gates can be connected to create a latch for storing data. As can be seen each of the gates are wired into the other inputs, meaning that once a gate receives an input value; it is possible to create a connection between the Vcc and ground. This connection can remain on even after the input source is released. Here the logic gate is connected through the D input and signals Q and $\overline{Q}$ are used as two outputs.

1.4.2 Using logic gates to store binary

There are actually three main types of latches which are used within circuit design. They all share the same principle to store a binary state inside the circuit. The SR latch will change from binary on or off each time the input to the circuit is connected. For instance if the input connection switches on, the state of the output will change to a 1 or on. The second time the input is connected the output will change to 0. The point of this is that the circuit is able to memorise the input. Meaning that even if the input is not connected the circuit still has a binary value 1 output. This is the principle in which data is stored within the circuit of a computer. This will usually be held within registers which contain 8 bits of data meaning that the circuit will have 8 small circuits which act as latches. Below shows a circuit of logic gates made from dozens of tiny transistors.

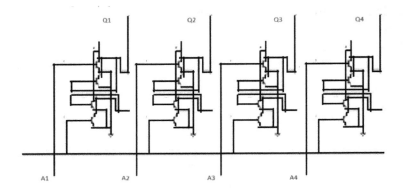

Fig: 1.4.2 A 4 bit register seen as a transistor circuit

1.4.3 Types of latch design

As mentioned, creating a latch allows a circuit to store a small amount of data. This can be useful when creating conditional functions which need to indicate if a criterion has been met. For instance a program might need to compare two strings of data and commit to a separate program if both strings of binary share the same output. Here a latch might be triggered on if this condition is true. Which will allow the program to move onto the second part of the sequence. This example would only need a latch which could store one or two bytes of information. When considering larger functions like registers or memory. The latches need to be larger in size and contain longer chains of transistor logic. The idea is that each part of the memory can be accessed as an input or output depending on the process which is occurring on the board.

It is important to describe how these circuits appear within circuit design. As it is possible to determine form the IC or logic gate connection what the circuit is trying to achieve. Below is a diagram of a 4 input quadruple D latch. This is primarily the main type of latch used within digital systems, as it is easily possible to change the input connection on the IC to connect to the board. If this is seen on a circuit design it usually refers to a memory system or register. The IC chip here would usually be used as 4 bytes used as memory within computers register.

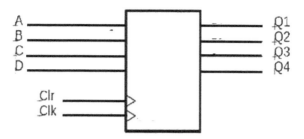

Fig: 1.4.3 Quadruple input D Flip Flop

1.5.1 Applications of digital logic systems

The chapter has tried to point out a number of ways in which network and circuit connections on a board can be applied in a meaningful way to subsystems and digital applications. For instance, digital logic can be used to create pathways which allow a CPU etc. to perform calculations and perform complex programs. It is also possible to create data applications which store information in the form of binary, through connecting logic gates. This is widely used in data manipulation as information can accessed and stored, as well as modified while in use. In fact there are many applications which use combinational digital logic and it is highly versatile for creating components which can be programmed and conduct numerous functions. For this reason understanding some of the basic principles of combinational logic are valuable when designing digital systems.

In fact within a computer system there are many processes which use specific forms of logic to create complex procedures. A MUX is probably the simplest form of digital logic as it can interpret the connections between two devices, or interfaces. A further development of this is a FPGA which has a number of digital connections, designed to perform a complex procedure. Graphical mapping between 16 and 256 bit can be utilised through this type of circuit. To develop this idea further below is a table with a number of computer processes which all use digital logic systems to perform a function.

TYPES OF DIGITAL LOGIC CIRCUITS

MUX	Encoder
FPGA	Decoder
MEMORY	Calculation
DATA DRIVERS	

Table: 1.5.1 Uses of digital logic in computers

1.6.1 Interpreting digital logic systems

This book will primarily look at the application of digital logic in computer processing. The emphasis is to understand how simple processes which a computer carries out are designed within an electrical basis. For instance a process such as computer calculation can be seen at the level of transistor connections. There will be a number of registers which contain a binary number and a sequence of logic gates which can perform a mathematical function on the input. It is at first not obvious how these events take place. Yet the connections which exist on the circuit can be recreated and tested as a number of transistor connections. The idea for the book will be to understand how these processes work, and then design some of the systems using an electronic design format. The idea is that the processes will be explained and then designed, from an electrical engineering perspective.

End of Chapter Quiz

How are digital systems designed?

How many types of truth table can you describe?

Why are latches used as memory?

Which type of digital logic is used in audio processing?

Digital Circuits with Memory

In this chapter you will look at the following

- Uses and functions
- Types of memory systems
- Designing a memory block
- Interfacing memory structures

2.1.1 Why do we use memory in a computer?

Combination logic is able to create a number of structures inside a computer, such as arithmetic, video processing and data analysis. These types of structures are essential for the functions which a computer is able to carry out, in fact the processes decide how a computer is expected to work. Another structure which a computer needs is a memory system. This is used to store the operating system, or smaller chunks of memory to load parts of the program for use during a routine's procedure. In today's computers there are many types of memory systems in use, these can be very small in size or contain huge amounts of information like todays ROMs. These now consist of large amounts of data cells which are so vast in size it can store and retrieve millions of bytes of information.

Traditionally computer systems where categorised into two formal types of processing systems. A digital system would be classed as an old Harvard system which used a digital circuit, such as an input and output device around a central processing unit. This type of system would be able to process information and the result would be then outputted onto the correct device or display. The Harvard system is used in circuits which are quite basic and act more as a complex electrical structure. An old relay system could be designed in such a way. The Von Neumann method is used to describe computerised structures which use a form of memory as well as input and output devices. These types of devices need to be designed to allow a system to store and retrieve information which the computer has been able to access or process

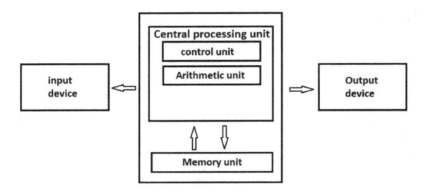

Fig: 2.1.1 Block diagram of a Von Neumann structure

In fact memory is essential to the procedures inside a computer, as systems need to be designed to store information and be able to process the information retrieved from other sources. The applications of the Von Neumann methods have allowed digital systems to contain operating systems which allow the 'user' an interface for the computers programmes. These systems are also able to store the code which programmes themselves need to create the routines. The Von Neumann method of electrical circuit design creates the core of today's computer systems.

TYPES OF DIGITAL MEMORY SYSTEMS AND USES

REGISTERS	Programming
RAM/ROM	Operating systems
CACHE	Routine clauses
FLAGS AND CATCHES	Call and jump instructions

Table: 2.1.1 Memory types and uses

The main advantages of the Von Neumann method of computerised circuits are that a computer is able to create a program and conduct a number of routines, which allow a programme to perform. The programme is obviously written onto the memory where it is accessed by the computers structure, and contains the processes written as code. Programming and software design is the main advantages of this type of model, as computer processes are able to be re written and designed around one system. For example a computer can be programmed to complete a multitude of tasks, and create new parameters with which it can function. The use of programming has allowed computing to achieve more depth due to the complexity which can be achieved by the software and written computer instructions.

2.1.2 Memory applications

Memory works by storing data in the form of bytes inside latches or memory cells. These cells can contain the information which the programme moves around. For instance when a computer forms a calculation such as the addition of two numbers, the binary will be stored in each of the registers and the result applied to the accumulator. This is actually a type of memory structure, despite being only a small process. Another component which uses memory is the ROM. This will contain the entirety of the programme needed for the calculation to be completed and the result displayed as an output etc. depending on the type of programme. Each of these functions would need a small amount of memory to work, or the computers' structure would forget what information it had been trying to process. The memory captures the information as it moves around the circuit.

There are two perspectives to take with the application of memory. An electrical viewpoint determines how the structures are designed and how the parts are interfaced for them to work. The other viewpoint of the memory design, would be how the computers software is expected to function. For example during a process, how much space is needed to move data and how many bytes of the data bus are expected to convert the instructions? These types of questions are essential to the design and function of the entire system. The design of the circuitry is based around aspects which consider these viewpoints of the entire system for it to work. The main consideration is what the system is trying to do.

2.2.1 Types of memory systems (registers)

The types of memory system determine the size of the storage and how it is to be designed. For instance a register would usually be designed around the size of the data carried across the data bus. If information was completed in 8 bytes per instruction, the register would need to be at least 8 bytes in size. The CPU would usually have a number of register banks, which could access the data bus and store a word or chunk of bytes of information. The design of the register would change if the component needed access to the ALU (calculation device) or the memory etc, as the register would need to transfer information between these processes. For instance the CPU inside the Z80 had 8 registers, which were used for memory, addressing, calculations and I/O connections. The registers are where the CPU does the bulk of its processing and stores the information before storage or interface outputs.

To explain the system inside the register further it is necessary to look at the diagram for the connections inside the circuit. The principle behind how the register works is storing a number of binary data inside a latch. When a register receives a signal across the data bus the register which is selected will store the binary until it is required to move to a different part of the program's procedure. The latch itself is designed by using a number of logic gates which store a byte each time it receives an on signal. The SR flip flop is the most commonly used latch as the connections of the gates are the easiest circuits to work with during design. Below shows the circuit for the SR flip flop as a number of transistors. These are the circuits which the logic gates represented in chapter 1. As can be seen the circuit needs a Vcc source and has a simple input and output. The input SR only needs to be on once the clock changes the state of the input.

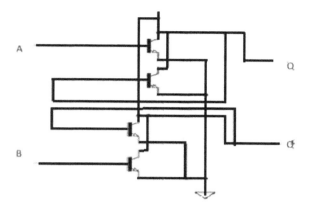

Fig: 2.2.1 Transistor connections for SR Flip Flop

The design of the latch can also be applied to the connections inside a register as the connections of the circuit can be repeated and used to make a number of latches which are able to store a number of bytes of information, used within the system. Here is another diagram of a register constructed from a number of SR Latches which are able to input 4 bits of information. The idea of the design is simple as the bytes are merely stored and the register has access to other systems so that the information can be moved on or processed depending on the program.

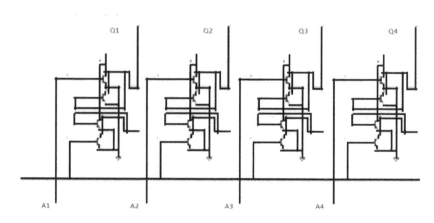

Fig 2.2.1 Transistor connections of a 4 bit register.

This simple diagram explores how a computer system might be designed to store 4 bits of data. The principle can be repeated on larger systems such as 8 or 16 bytes using the same procedure. The idea is that the logic gates can be replaced by the application of a number of transistors, which are able to mimic the circuit

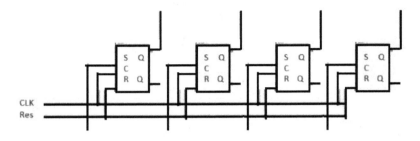

Fig: 2.2.1 Circuit diagram of a 4 bit D Flip Flop

2.2.2 Stack and Jump procedures

Due to the way data is moved the register is usually the same size as the data bus, as the design of the register is used in a number of other procedures. Processes such as the stack and the instruction register often need to contain the information contained on the data bus and store this temporarily. As the information contained on the bytes can be held and decoded across this system. These kinds of structures can be created using d flip flop chips, again made from a number of transistors connected across the circuit. They would be designed in exactly the same way except the output from the circuit would be directly connected to the decoder or system it is interfaced with. The connections of the circuit determine how the register would then function. In fact due to the similarity of different registers, many types of systems can be replaced by using the RAM as a number of different registers. For instance the stack on most of today's chips are held within a memory location rather than a different system. This means making a board will contain fewer systems, and a greater number of addressing procedures.

2.3.1 Designing a memory block

Memory storage such as RAM or ROM are designed differently than registers, as they are used by different structures inside the system. A register will usually be contained in the CPU, while the ROM will be based in a separate chip or system. This is due to the design and uses of this type of component. Although the design is based on a similar set of connections. Both systems use latches to store the binary and they are accessed and function in a similar way. A memory system will hold large blocks of memory that contain bytes of information stored in words. A 16 bit computer will have memory which contains the data in groups of 16 bytes. For instance a 64K memory will have each instruction held in block of 16 bytes. The data can be accessed across the data bus in 16 bytes. This is a typical representation of memory and describes the way in which the design of the memory is connected.

The structure of large memory cells behaves a lot like a number of registers, which have access to the data bus each time the word is connected across the circuit. This is represented on the diagram below which at first looks like a register as it is connected in almost the same way as was seen before. The difference is that this circuits will be repeated hundreds of times and allow large numbers of cells to contain information which acts as a memory. Another difference is that the connections contain a further input which is accessed by the address bus each time the cell is in use. For instance the address bus will point to the cell reference and read or write to the memory cell depending on which function of the memory is being utilised by the CPU at that point in the program.

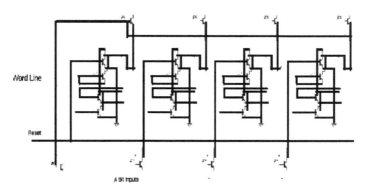

Fig: 2.3.1 Transistor connections of a ROMS memory cell

Here the cells in the memory are connected across a number of circuits which the address bus can access each time the stack pointer locates the next address. The stack pointer will be able to determine each separate cell of memory, which in turn is sent to the instruction register for decoding. The connections can actually be made in any way, but this design allows for an idea of how the circuit might actually look.

2.3.2 DRAM and SRAM memory

As can be seen a standard memory cell can be made from the wiring of a number of transistors. When connected in a group of latches it is possible to store and load information in to the circuit's structure. There are actually a number of ways in which a memory cell can be configured as the type designed here is outdated due to the number of components needed and also the overall size of the design. Memory which uses a cell of transistors, is considered to be classed as SRAM. These types of components are better at information but are also difficult to build. Since the design of this type of system, the SRAM has been replaced with newer techniques which are easier to construct and smaller in size, meaning being capable of higher numbers of memory blocks. The diagram below shows a memory block of cells using DRAM.

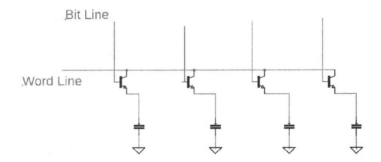

Fig: 2.3.2 DRAM memory cell using capacitors

DRAM is made from the composition of fewer number of transistor gates and the addition of a number of capacitors which store the binary. This means the part is magnetised into holding the information, rather than using latches to create an open circuit. There are many advantages of using this type of technique and are mainly found in more modern computers.

2.4.1 Chip timing the read/ write cycle

Throughout the circuit of the computers wiring board, the system is constantly manipulating the contents across the data and address buses. There are a number of complicated processes which occur at the same and for this reason there are a number of procedures which share the bus. During the cycle each component waits for other processes to occur, before carrying out the next procedure. All of these processes are conducted by the use of a single timer clock which creates the on off values between instruction cycles. The clocks timer will be wired into each chip or component, allowing the next process to occur. The use of the clock cycle means that each event inside a programme occurs without interfering with the events of another component or chip. This creates the fluid uses of the electrical mechanisms of the computer, without stalling or crashing the programme.

The timing events which occur across the timing cycles merely allow for the uses of the data bus, identifying which chip needs access to the bus at any particular time. Whereas other processes which are timed on the board, allow a system to perform a small routine before completing an event. The actual timing of each part of the computer is known as the instruction cycle and the computer will conduct one process across however many number of on and off. Some program cycles are small, such as one or two processes between instructions, where as some designs need many more processes per instruction cycle. For the routine to perform the procedure. The memory R/W is one of these types of processes. For example a computer may have 5 steps per instruction and the R/W cycle needs to clear the cache before loading the memory contents. The R/W cycle identifies the time of this process.

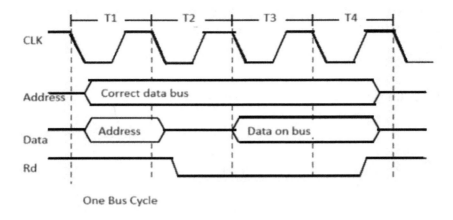

Fig: 2.4.1 Memory R/W cycle

As can be seen from the diagram, the address is read from the memory at the first two clock pulses of the instruction cycle. The data is then transferred during the final two stages of the cycle's process. Here the data would use the data bus to identify the relevant system. This is useful to understand when creating the fetch decode cycle, or when creating the parameters of the instruction registers. The diagram here shows the timing cycle for a ROM (read only) component as there is actually no write instruction during this process. The instruction cycle is also four clock pulses in length. A similar diagram for a RAM component would also contain the parameters for the write instruction, where the binary is actually stored in the memory cell within the address block.

2.5.1 Interfacing memory

A computer system formerly has two types of memory. The read only memory which contains the programs, and the random access which stores information temporarily during routines and cycles. Although it is possible to count all memory as one set of memory which has been split into a number of parts, one for each type of process. The reason for this is that the memory has to be accessed through the same number of address ports. Below identifies the memory location of four parts of memory. Yet each part on the board is located in different locations.

$0-$7FFF = ROM
$8000 - $9FFF = RAM
$B000 - $CFFF = Sound
$D000 - $FFF = Display

These may be split further into other blocks such as stack and registers used for creating parameters. Depending on the wiring this could be completed across a number of chips or in different components across the board. For this reason the interfacing of the memory poses a number of difficulties when considering how the chips are connected. The main point to consider is the control of the timing cycle and the connection going to and from the address bus. The picture below shows how a ROM chip can be wired to allow the memory to be written on.

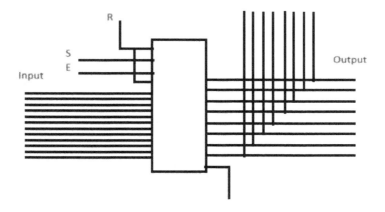

Fig: 2.5.1 writing to a ROM chip

As can be seen from the diagram the chip has a number of connections which allow for the timing of the chip as well a connection to the address and data bus. When writing to the chip the address bus will select the point in the memory, allowing the data bus to input the binary. Once stored the data bus is then used as an output port. Meaning that the data will only be sent across in one direction during the read cycle. The change of the procedure of the chip is completed by allowing a signal source to the chip enable pin as well as the R/W pin. This is due to the ring of the chip allowing access to the memory cells structure. Although this diagram identifies how to program a ROM. These types of chips are usually made using a PAL component which directly writes onto the surface of the chip's components. Saving time and allowing the computer to function at a higher rate of performance.

End of Chapter Quiz

Do Harvard systems use software?

Identify three structures which use binary storage?

Why do some memory cells use DRAM?

What does ROM stand for?

Instructions and Addressing

In this chapter you will look at the following

- Instruction sets and their uses
- Designing a set of instructions
- Creating complex instructions through functions
- Fetch decode cycle
- Addressing modes

3.1.1 An overview of instruction sets

A fundamental part of software programming is the use of instruction sets to create a routine or programme. Instructions are used by the computer to infer a process. For instance a computer may be able to perform a number of move instructions between registers. What this means is that the computer or instruction decoder is designed to allow the computer to move binary information between registers in a number of ways. The code below shows a few instructions written in asm.

```
Mov A, 25
Mov B, 56
Mov A, B
```

The above code represents 3 instructions which move information between registers A and B. The first line will move 25 decimal into the register. The second instruction is similar and completes the same process for register B. The last instruction exchanges the values between the two registers. This is an example of a set of instructions which the computer is programmed to perform. A computer is actually able to complete as many instructions which are available on the bandwidth of the addressing bus, although not all computers use all of the space provided. The Z80 had 16 bits of instruction space and of which nearly 516 instructions were available to create a programme with.

A computer routine functions by calling one set of instructions after another. During the compiling of the programme the computer should be able to complete a routine depending on the purpose of the programme. Consider the following code, again it is written in asm.

```
Mov A, 6
Mov B, 3
Add A, B, D
```

This set of instruction moves the data into the registers and performs a calculation function to add the two registers. This completes the routine and the result is displayed in register D. This is obviously a very simple instruction but proves that by compiling groups of instructions together it is possible to create a programme. To use this example in a 16 bit machine, it would be possible to call a number of these functions which would then form the basis of the calculator software. The system would use each instruction to decode the various command prompts. Basically the instructions form the processes which the computer is able to carry out.

3.1.2 Creating groups of instructions

Instruction sets can usually be grouped around certain processes. Some instructions might be used for calculations. Other instructions might be useful to complete call and jump functions, which would be useful for conditional formatting in some software. This is due to the design of a computer; from an electrical perspective the computer needs to be able to complete the greatest number of instructions and be as easy to wire as possible. For this reason the instructions are usually grouped around a number of premises which the computer is designed to achieve. For instance a computer may be graphical, this would mean that the computer is able to manipulate graphic files. Another computer might be used for storage and data manipulation. For this reason it would need more instructions which serve the purpose of calculating large bytes of data. The registers would have to be larger and the computer able to complete more functions

During the design of a computer it is useful to perceive how the computer is going to work and what processes the computer will complete. To explain this point the following table lists a few examples of the processes of an ALU. This explains what the computers calculator is able to achieve.

BASIC ALU INSTRUCTIONS	
ADD	increment
SUBTRACT	shift
MULTIPLY	Bit compare
DIVIDE	

Table: 3.1.2 basic instructions in an ALU

Here the computer has a number of instructions which forms the basis of the calculator during a programme or routine. The instructions can be used in any program, as well as the calculator as the instruction sets are not specific to just one format. Many types of programmes need to use instructions such as compare and increment for them to work. The idea is that the instructions create the best functionality of the machine.

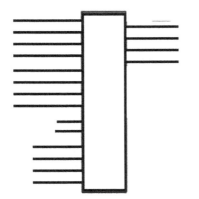

S INPUT	COMMAND
0001	ADD
0010	SUB
0011	MULT
0100	DIVD
0101	COMP
0110	INC
0111	DECRE
1000	SHIFT

Fig: 3.1.2 An ALU design with a truth table stating the instruction sets

3.1.3 Designing a set of instructions

The purpose of grouping instructions is due to how the computer is designed. It needs to understand which set of processes are used for different parts of command routines. The ALU will have a number of specific instructions, whereas the register, and stack will also have their own set due to the conditions under which the computer will work. It is important concept to understand during design as the register and the ALU will need to be electronically configured to complete these parameters, once a clear design for the computer has been met. The computer will only be able to complete these commands, as they are hard wired and determine how the system functions. Once hard written the computer will only be able to understand and process information in this way

CALL, JUMP INSTRUCTIONS	
CALL	Push stack
JUMP	Pop stack
RETURN	Bit skip if set
JUMP WHEN ZERO	Bit skip if zero

Table: 3.1.2 basic instructions for conditional sequences

Above is another table for instruction which can be used for conditional jump sequences during a routine. This set of instructions would allow the programme to call a function and return back to the main part of the programme. Which would allow a programme more dynamics in terms of interrupts and extra sequences. Designing this part of the computer would mean that the program counter and stack would need to be hard wired to call an address in memory when a routine is pushed into the stack register. In fact all of the instructions would need to have an electrical basis or the instruction would simply not work. Meaning that the computer has to contain the circuits to run these instructions.

The purpose of grouping instruction sets is to understand what the computer is able to do, and also for the use of the electrical engineer to wire each system into the design of the component

3.1.4 Creating functions out of small sets of parameters

The instructions which were used on the ALU might seem a little basic as the ALU is only performing four or five sets of instructions and a computer is able to complete more than dozens of routines. In fact the ALU does not need hundreds of instructions as it is possible to create functional parameters inside a routine which are able to perform complex tasks by changing the instructions parameters. For instance the divide was originally designed as the document for Euclid's theory of subtraction. Where the divisor of a number is repeatedly removed form a dividend, until there is no longer a further whole number. Take the following example.

Dividend 7, Divisor 3

```
Ld A, 7              //Load D
Mov B, 3             //Divisor
Mov C, 7             //Loop counter

SUBTRACT
Sub A,B
Dec C
Compare C,0
BTSCC                //Jump if value is not 0
Jump SUBTRACT

CHECK DIV
Sub D,C              // find how many times the divisor has counted
Store accumulator

return

END
```

The code is able to complete a divide instruction by repeatedly subtracting the same number until the counter reaches zero. This programme is an example of using a small number of instructions to create a function. In fact many types of programmes can be completed by manipulating a functions parameter which works by changing the use of a set of instructions. These types of processes allow a programmer more functionality from machines which are restricted in terms of their uses. Programs can use these types of effects to achieve more complex programs from restricted instruction sets. Lambda equations are used in programming mathematical formulas, when a computer is unable to create the sequences needed to perform certain types of processes.

3.2.1 The fetch execute cycle

So far, we have explained what an instruction set is and how they are used by the computer during the run time of a program. The instructions will be read by the memory and decoded by the instruction register before moving on to the next set of instructions. This would also signal an increment to the program counter which will read the next part of the memory. The process of the instruction being read by the instruction register is termed the fetch execute cycle. To understand this process further it is necessary to explain how an opcode and operand work in terms of the binary reference. Below shows a diagram of a number in binary which would be held within the memory before being decoded. This is usually 8 to 64 bits in length, and is split in two parts. One part would be the instruction and the other the data which the instruction refers to. Sometimes this part is blank if there is no data used in the operand, depending on the system which is being used.

Mov A, 255

OPCODE		OPERAND	
0110	1010	0000	255

Fig: 3.2.1 an instruction seen as an op code and operand

As can be seen from the diagram the instruction has two parts which are received by the CPU and decoded. This is completed by the instruction decoder inside the processor. The processor will usually have an address line which is 16 bits in length and a data out. The address line is where the

16 bits of data are decoded. Consider the following example of two lines of code, both of which have an opcode and operand.

Mov B, 255   0000 0110 1111 1111

Mov A, 55   0000 0101 0011 0111

    Here the code is written in two parts, the first 8 bits are similar as the opcode completes the same function as the first. The last 8 digits are data as the binary takes the form of a number. This part will be the information in the instruction which is the data. When the code is sent to the CPU the first 8 bytes are decoded and the second 8 bytes are reserved for data pathways in the circuitry. The instruction merely sends a binary value into a register. To explore this process in more detail here is a diagram of an instruction being read by the system as it is decoded and carried out.

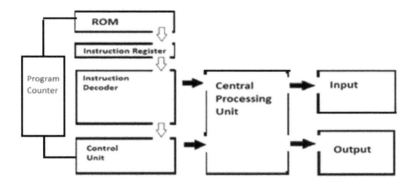

Fig 3.2.1 Diagram of an instruction being processed.

3.2.2 Decoding an instruction

    The process of the fetch cycle is controlled by the circuits inside the CPU. The control unit determines which part of the system has access to the data bus at any time. Which is determined by a timing signal changing the state of the data bus. The control unit works in a number of stages. Usually between T0 – T5 each phase designates a different stage on the control unit. During the first timing signals or fetch stage the control unit receives the instruction from memory and sends this across to the instruction register where it is decoded. The second stage of the cycle is where the instruction is executed by the circuitry in the CPU where the purpose of the instruction has been performed, meaning that the programme can run onto the next instruction. The final stage of the cycle increments the counter which means that the memory pointer is ready at the next location on the ROM. Below shows the stages which the control unit completes as it moves through the timing cycle.

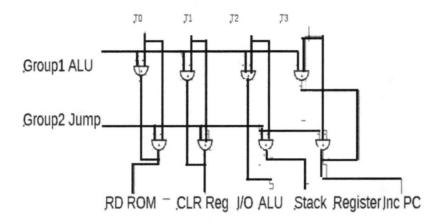

Fig: 3.2.1 the phases of control unit

The stages which the control unit completes is actually made of a timing signal and a number of logic gates which coordinate the instruction being read at any particular time. The timer moves throughout each phase T0- T5 and providing a signal to different outputs depending on the instruction. The instruction or instruction group will determine the network which the control signal will operate. For instance all calculation signals will move a part of the memories register into the data bus of the ALU. Whereas instructions which access the stack and program counter are wired to a different part of the system and only have access to these parts. To make the processes inside the control unit simpler it is possible to create a group of instructions which the control unit can understand rather than a process for each different instruction.

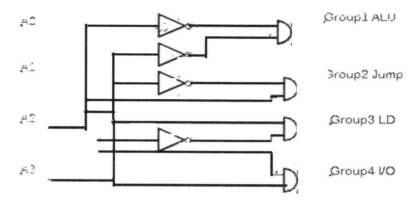

Fig 3.2.1: Grouping instruction sets into hot codes

3.3.1 Addressing modes

The concept varies between devices as computers use different techniques to store and retrieve data. As the main focus of the text is to explore wiring of a computer, I will try to explain how a computer uses a number of different modes to perform and conduct the instructions or routines. Literally speaking an addressing mode can be how a computer is able to infer a data address. For example

Mov 1234, D0   or
Mov D0, A2.

Here the instruction seems to be completing exactly the same task which is moving 16 byte value into another location. These are actually two ways of performing a similar programme. The reason being that the first line of code is telling the computer to move the contents of location 1234 and place this in register D0. The second line of code tells the computer to move the contents between registers. From a coding perspective it seems that the computer should automatically be able to complete these two separate functions. What is actually happening is that the programme requires access to the memory address in the first reference but only the registers in the next line of code.

The reason for this is that the two examples refer to two different variations of addressing modes. Computers are able to complete routines in a number of ways and have a multitude of addressing modes, with which to undergo a routine. Within direct addressing the actual memory location will be referenced, whereas with Indirect addressing works between registers. The topic can be quite important to understanding and developing coding strategies. As only some types of coding definitions are actually possible. As the code needs to relate to the wiring which exists on the CPU. The CPU is actually designed in such a way with which it is possible to only complete certain tasks due to formatting of the connections which exist on the chip. This is something which is important to understand in the designing of computerised instruction sets.

For example to simplify the design of the computer, some wiring exists only on the CPU, such as movement between registers. On other types of instructions, the CPU has to load information to circuits outside of the processor which means it needs access to the data bus. For this reason the instruction decoder will need to respond in different ways for the procedure to be completed. To minimise the circuitry needed for these types of routines. The processor is expected to have only a few types of different connections, which are able to carry out the same routine under different conditions. Meaning that addressing modes that access the memory need to complete a process which uses the control bus to find a memory address location. Effectively being a different process to a register movement instruction.

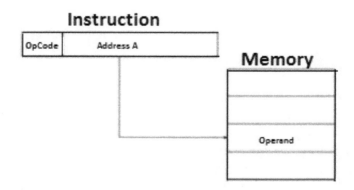

Fig: 3.4.1 example of direct addressing

3.4.2 Further instruction parameters

It is possible to use addressing modes to explore how a computer works while it is decoding an instruction. As the processor not only decodes the information, it actually needs to interpret how the binary is expected to work. Specifying the differences in locating data stored in different locations is one example of instruction decoding. During the fetch execute cycle the instruction decoder and control unit are responsible for interpreting the binary instruction, and allowing the data to pass across the bus. We have already looked at the binary instruction as a number of parts, i.e. an opcode an operand. This is a simplified way of how an instruction works, as the binary can be interpreted differently according to the type of instruction sent. Obviously, some data has no form of opcode, such as sound processing. Also some instructions use a greater number of binary definitions. This is dependent on the program and how the CPU is designed.

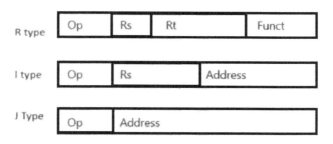

Fig 3.4.2: Parameters for instruction set decoding

To explain this further it is possible to point out three types of instruction translations. The first being reserved for arithmetic, which allows the data to be spilt across three different registers specific to data manipulations. This type of instruction splits 64 bytes into an op code the content of each register and the function. This is considered an instruction sent through the CPU as an R type. The second types of instruction are used for movement between registers, here the instruction is again split between a segment for the opcode another for the registers or address. This is slightly different to the first as the bytes sequence would be read by the processor in its own context. This is considered I types addressing. The final types of addressing are for jump sequences. The instruction merely needs and opcode and the address of the location to jump to. The below diagram, explains how each type of code would be written in bytes.

End of Chapter Quiz

Why is it important to categorise instruction types?

Which component controls the fetch cycle?

How does a function work?

Name three types of instruction formats?

Procedures, Datasets and Routines

In this chapter you will look at the following

- Routines and subroutines
- Programme sequences and branching
- Creating procedures and functions
- Using data sets to search and query

4.1.1 Understanding how a programme works

A computer is a procedure-based calculator, it has the ability to move information from the memory and compile the data by sorting and retrieving relevant code from the CPU. Due to the connections inside the computer being a number of complex networks. The computer has to think in stages and works by sorting the data in one set of groups after the other. For instance the memory of the machine will have a number of lines of code written in a hex format. The system then allows each part of hex to work in turn. This process is why early programmes work in a sequence of procedures one stage after the other. Programmes combine a number of techniques to allow software to retrieve and sort information into relevant contexts for the 'user'. These techniques involve the use of creating meaningful datasets to store information, and processes which the 'user' is able to apply to manipulating code.

The essence of programming is to create a number of routines which determines how the programme functions, as it runs through the procedures. The programme may consist of any number of formats such as data storage, arithmetical methods or responses to commands etc. Yet there are a number of underlying processes which determine how the programme would be written or coded for the overall structure to work. The aim of the chapter is to determine a number of underlying principles inside computer programming, which will be able to clarify how to build the machine from an electrical engineering perspective.

4.1.2 Using a flow chart to determine a simple process.

A programme would work by adhering to a number of steps or stages which work one after the other. The computer will infer the instructions from each stage before moving onto the next process. For instance the calculation of two number might take the format of the following code.

```
Mov A, 56
Add A, 255
```

This is simply adding two values together, the code also might need to read an I/O port which would slightly change the code to:

```
Read D,
LD A
Add 255
```

This describes a small calculation process which a simple computer is able to achieve. A programme would usually need a lot more complexity for it to work. The program might for instance have a user interface for commanding inputs, or a number of processes it is able to infer. The calculator should be able to achieve more than just addition, and need other set of commands. If we plotted this scenario into a flow chart. It is possible to understand how the programme works and the stages which the computer needs to work through for the programme to run.

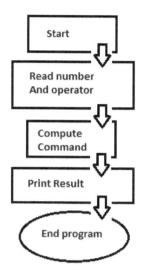

Fig 4.1.2: Flow chart for simple calculator

Here the programme works by the 'user' defining two numbers and the type of calculation to process, the result is then written onto the screen. This programme is quite straight forward as the command only has only a few inputs and variables with which to work with, and the routine simple runs the data based on the commands chosen by the users' interface. If we look at this process as an asm document it is possible to see how the computer might be instructed to perform this procedure. For instance a program might work in the following format.

```
Input:
Read d                //Read the input status
Ld a
Read d
Ld b

Calculate:
Check bit 1
Jz MathAdd            //jump to procedure
Check bit 2
Jz MathSub            //jump to procedure
```

```
SaveResult:
Store Acc, 0x64
Jr Print

MathAdd:                    //run procedure
Ld a, Acc
Add b
Jr SaveResult

MathSub:                    //run procedure
Ld a, Acc
Sub b
Jr SaveResult

Print:
Ld Acc 00X6400             //print result on segment display
```

Here a calculation is performed on the inputs from the data bus and the output printed on a part of the memory address dedicated to the LCD screen. The program runs in sequence except for the few commands which allow the program to jump between subroutines. This forms the basis of the entire programme, which allows the user to perform either command of addition or subtraction. The program is adaptation of the flowchart but could be written in any number of ways.

4.1.3 Why do we use flow charts

The reason a programme is written into a flow chart is that the structure of a program might have a number of sequences and branches which affect how the programme develops. For instance a programme for a robot describing the dimensions of an object might have a number of conditional sequences, which allow sensors to coordinate motors to move around the object. Due to the conditional parameters of movement the programme would branch and develop depending on how the inputs are interpreted by the programme's instructions. A flow chart allows a developer to understand the processes of the programme and identifies how the code needs to look, for the programme to be effectively carried out. Also it is easier to check errors at this stage rather than during the compiling of code.

4.1.4 Sequences and branches

As can be seen the sequences and branches which exist on a programme are easily visible, and it is possible to observe how the programme might respond under a number of conditions. The programme still develops by running through each part in order but creates branches when the code responds to interrupts or conditional responses. For instance the following code represents a conditional statement which checks two parameters:

```
Var Name Int
Procedure () Name
Read string Input

If Name.Space <=3 or >20
Print String "Name bust be shorter than 20 letters"
Else Print name
```

Here the programme has two outputs which make the programme branch to another response depending on the inputted values name space. This is an example of when a sequence branches into a number of outputs, changing the way the programme runs. From a design perspective. The computer would have to be able to jump to another part of the programme when a certain parameter or condition is met. The programme needs to be able to perform a jump command to complete this routine. This is achieved during the compiling of the programme as the memory pointer is located at this name space and jumps when prompted to a different part of the programme. The entire programme is still completed in a number of lines of Hex, which continue to run in sequence.

TYPES OF FUNCTIONS USED IN CONDITIONAL SEQUENCES

CALL	Less/ greater than
JUMP	And/ or functions
ELSE/IF	Compare
FOR/ WHILE LOOP	Jump when zero

Table 4.1.4 types of functions used in conditional statements

4.2.1 Routines and subroutines

Conditional branches and sequence allow a programme to complete the processes and react to a number of different prompts and commands; which makes the structure more dynamic and fluid to different events. These techniques work alongside call functions and subroutines. These can be made up of small chunks of programming which the routine calls on occasion throughout the run time of the entirety of the process. For instance in the above example there are a number of small commands prompts which call upon a small subroutine to complete a process. MathAdd, MathSub and SaveResult where all examples of a specified call instruction, which then jumps to the subroutine and then to either a Return value where it would remember the location in the program or jump to another instruction depending on the type of routine being carried out.

The way this works is that instead of the call function being coded, what is written on the memory of the computer is the actual memory address of the start of the routine. For instance the following code would be interpreted by the compiler as a memory address.

FindRectangle
Read D
Ld a
RotateSensor
Read D
Ld B

```
PrintArea
Area = a*b
return
```

Here for instance the memory interprets this instruction RotateSensor as a call function and jumps to the location of the memory which this instruction is written. This process is completed by the Stack pointer and the addressing found in the program counter. This allows the program to jump between points and commit to different tasks. The stack and the PC are responsible for these types of tasks.

4.3.1 Using functions and procedures to create routines

There is now almost enough information to get a computer to run a dynamic programme. However the parts listed so far of a programme only commit to the overall structure. This may be only needed during the design phase, where the arguments which underpin the routine are created in concept and designed as a template or idea. The code itself would take the form of a number of functions and procedures which develop processes which manipulate data.

To explain this idea in a little more detail we could create a program which uses distances to create vectors to use for potential pathways for navigation. A computer could be used to interpret which direction to travel depending on the distances in direction and height that are given to a specific point. The program would need to read information from the sensors and determine the fastest methods of travel. The computer takes the information from the sensors and moves the vehicle into the specified trajectory. To complete this process the computer would need a number of procedures and mathematical functions such as:

```
ReadHeighDistance
CalculateTrajectory
CoordiatePath
```

The Procedure read height and distance would need a number of functions which could calculate the distance travelled once the height and length of journey are recorded. The parameters would merely take the information from the sensors and use the inputs to return a value measured in meters etc. For instance

ReadSensors

Rd D // Sensor height
Ld A
Rd E // Sensor distance
Ld b
Multiply a,b
Multiply Acc, 1.001 // convert to meters
Store 0x4F

Return

CommitMovement
Ld F, 0x4F // Move memory location to motors output

Here the procedure is carried out by completing a number of functions which allow the computer to return a value in meters which is able to interpret the distance a motor might need to travel. This allows the computer to understand how a journey would be considered by a computer's internal mechanisms. The procedure works by encapsulating the processes into a number of small call routines. Inside a programme or piece of code there would be dozens of routines and procedures which use the functions of the processor to create the software process. This is important to understand, due to the methods of designing a computer. The computer needs to be able run the desired software, and the hardware need to be able to perform the necessary functions of each stage of the routine. The networks and circuitry have to be able to complete the required processes for it to work.

4.4.1 Using a dataset to store information

Datasets come in a variety of types, they can be numerical or alphabetical, dependent on the type of information being used. Data types can also categorise items through reference, such as logging the number of items stored as cargo on a ship. If the items where categorised and counted this would be considered an example of a data set. A data set can take any type of form and is often used for mathematical or statistical analysis. These types of data contain numerical information which could be used to perform calculations. A data set is basically a list of information stored in categories which identify the type of items held. Data sets are used in many types of programs and these can perform function like search and retrieve to find information stored within these lists.

Here is an example of a dataset for reference which could be stored in memory in a number of ways. Each item could be loaded onto a separate hex format, each having its own address. It could also be stored in categories with markers, etc. depending on how the computer is designed to save information onto the RAM. The idea is that a relevant technique is used so that creating a CSV (command prompt) is relatively easy when querying the data. Below is a small data set used in early types of COBALT programmes.

Item No.	Type	Stock	Out	In
1	Barrel	5	3	2
2	Box	10	4	2
3	Tank	5	5	1
4	Cargo	15	5	4

Table 4.4.1 example of type of information held in a dataset

The first point to consider is the data types. These would be handled by different processes inside the computer. Number systems are different to word processes as the binary used to identify them is coded differently. Meaning that identifying each type of data would necessitate the computer performing separate processes when running a query. This would have to be taken into account when running the code. The rest of the data set is actually quite straight forward. It simply lists details held in stock of a number of items. The system is able to record the amounts of each type. To store this information would mean creating a list for each number stored within a range of addresses. The list when called could be used to populate each category which is being requested. The table would actually look like a list inside the memory.

1, Barrel, 5, 3, 2
2, Box, 10, 4, 2
3, Tank, 5, 5, 1
4, Cargo, 15, 5, 4

Depending on the design of the programme, the list would either be stored as a table, or in the form of a data set where items can be retrieved and used to calculate numerical assumptions. The purpose of the data set is to store numerical values so that the information can later be searched and retrieved through the use of creating a CSV query. The purpose of the programme is that it finds a way of searching the data and solving the query.

4.4.2 Why do we use datasets?

A data set is quite a basic construct inside a computer system, and the principle has been used in a number of programmes. By storing information in a dataset it is possible to manipulate the contents and perform calculations on the data. These types of procedures are able to provide detailed information which can be used in a number of formats. For instance the sales of a small business could be stored as numerical values of season and profit made. This could then be used to identify the averages of consumer trends over each month. This information would be useful for the purposes of industry, such as retailers waiting to make buy or sell their products. There are actually many uses for dataset, depending on the information stored and the programme which is being used to access the data

4.4.3 Using CSV functions to search, extract and create queries

If we use the example of the data set which had been created for a cargo ship. The information can be manipulated through the use of creating a CSV query. This is a type of programme which uses a function to retrieve information and display the data for the use of analysis. Types of query involve searching the data, finding information under a number of parameters or conditions, as well as listing information which belongs to certain categories. To understand this process further it would be useful to create a small programme which would identify some of the techniques the system uses to format the data. For instance in this query we want to identify each item of cargo which has more than five in stock.

The query might take the form of the following asm.

Find item stock level

```
Locate item
Mov 64, b              // locate start of data set

Finddata
Add 48,b Acc
Push stack, Acc        //find desired memory location of stock item
Pop Stack, a
Sub 5, a
Bit check Acc, 0000 0000
If set Call next item
Else print b
Ld a, 80               // load length of string

PrintString            //Print length of string
Inc b
Print b
Dec a
DJNZ, a
return

Item2
Move 64 b
Add 80
Call FindData

End program
```

This program could be easily simplified but it would return the following print out on a LCD display

1, Barrel, 5, 3, 2
2, Box, 10, 4, 2

This is due to the code searching the first two items on the list and printing out the response due to the cargo containing more than five items. The code is actually quite difficult to achieve and I have based this on a very simple 8 bit computerised system with only a small number of instructions. The idea is that this query would be able to function on a computer to retrieve information, the query would be used inside a CSV document to retrieve data. This could then be repeated on a format which uses the same memory addresses etc, and the code re run under different conditions. The idea is that the principle of the code reflects how the computer might actually work, and the types of processes it needs to achieve. The purpose of this is to understand how the circuitry of the computer might need to work based on the software it expects to incorporate.

For example navigating through the list would entail that the memory pointer has to jump between locations. Here the list might comprise of four sets of 16 byte memory cells. The CSV query merely prompts the stack to retrieve information between these locations

End of Chapter Quiz

Why does a programme need a structure?

What is the purpose of a routine?

Why do programmes use procedures and functions?

Identify a query which could be used on a dataset?

Part 2

Designing Structures in a Computer System

5

Simple ALUs

In this chapter you will look at the following

- The purpose of an ALU
- Understanding a simple ALU block diagram
- Identifying components inside an ALU
- Designing the processes for the module

5.1.1 What is an ALU in a processor?

We are now going to look at the processes and structures which exist inside a computer; in the hope that by describing the components and their circuitry, it is possible to design a computerised system. This could be done in a number of ways, but it possible to begin with the topic of an ALU. This is an abbreviation of the term Arithmetical Logic Unit. Which means it is the part of the computer which is responsible for creating the calculations and arithmetical responses which occur inside a CPU. When we usually consider the term of calculation device, we would assume that the only purpose for the device would be to assess formulas and respond to numbers and equations, as this is what the term means. This is not actually the case inside a computer, as the computer also needs this device to perform many other functions and processes. For example a jump or search instruction might actually need to use the ALU to perform these processes, meaning it is more functional than just simple calculations.

Fig 5.1.1 schematic diagram of an ALU

The ALU is designed around a number of processes which the CPU can use to perform calculations or arithmetic. In theory an ALU could perform any type of instruction, yet most ALUs are limited in terms of bit size meaning they are only able to complete a limited number of commands. For example a 4 bit ALU would only have the possibility of completing 16 different types of calculations. This might mean it is limited to only simple arithmetic, compare or logical functions. Although many computers install this type of logic as it is more than possible to create complicated software procedures with only this many instructions. In terms of reducing the design of the ALU this actually makes the process simpler, as it is possible to create a sophisticated computer which only needs a few instruction sets for it to work. As mentioned, a basic ALU will only need to handle arithmetic and logic statements to compete most of the work.

In terms of the structure of the computer the ALU is located inside the central processor. It is one of the most important parts of the component as it completes most of the processes which occur in the unit. Despite the necessity of the device the registers are the only other parts of the processor which it has access to. Usually there will be a number of registers which are able to transfer information to this unit. For instance on the Z80 there are two registers which are used specifically for data manipulation. Making the registers specific to the device. It is important to mention that the ALU will also have its own register known as an accumulator which would be used to store the results of the data. The CPU can then directly transfer this internally or to the outputs or memory.

5.1.2 Looking at a simple CPU

To understand the purpose of the ALU it is necessary to understand each of the processes it completes and how these are used inside a program. If we take a look at the figure below, this explains what functions the device can actually perform. The block diagram is taken from the processes which occur inside a basic 8 bit CPU and is actually quite simple to explain. This type of CPU has only a few types of instructions. Such as add, subtract, compare, increment and bit select. The Basic software language ran completely on this limited amount of instructions. Which were able to complete all the processes necessary for the computer's software. The language was designed around the functions which existed inside this unit. If we take a look at the diagram itself the unit is split into a number of parts. The first being the two input registers, which handle the data provided from the CPU. These allow 255 bytes of information per register, meaning that the computer cannot perform calculations which exceed this figure. These are used to store the numbers before they are used for calculation.

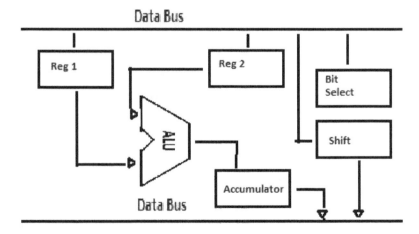

Fig 5.1.2 Block diagram of the ALU found in a basic CPU

How the registers work is through the application of a number of latches like we have seen described using the digital logic. These have 8 bytes which allow a small binary number to be stored before being passed onto the data bus. Depending on the type of instruction which is being decoded the information on the register will be processed by a number of different structures. The register again is a very simple structure which reacts like a small piece of memory. This can be rewritten and called on during any part of a procedure.

If we again look again at the block diagram, we can see that the registers are connected by a transfer latch which decides which process is being carried out. This is determined by the binary sent from the instruction to the MUX during the decode cycle. Each component has its own function. For example one part of the ALU complete an addition, while the ALU has a separate structure for incrementing the register. This is achieved by an internal address bus attached to each of the registers which feed directly into the component. The instruction being carried out depends on the control unit and the instruction being sent. The result of the calculation is then stored in the Accumulator before being sent across the data bus. The block diagram identifies some of the data transfer patterns which exist on the board.

TYPES OF ARITHMETIC FUNCTION

ADD/ SUBTRACT	Logic functions
SHIFT	Comparison
INCREMEMT	Decrement
BIT COMPARE	

Table 5.2.1 Types of CPU calculation instructions

5.2.1 Identifying structures on the ALU

Each function which the ALU is able to complete is carried out by a structure which manipulates the binary sent across the data bus. For instance the logical functions would have the circuitry which contained the digital logic able to complete the arithmetic. This is important in deciding on how to design the CPU as each instruction needs to be identified before a practical application is created as a circuit. For instance there are around eight functions which the ALU is able to complete, and for the computer to work the function would need its own form of circuitry. The actual circuits can be designed relatively easily through the use of connected transistors and comparator circuits.

5.2.2 Describing a simple circuit using a 1 bit adder

The addition function is one of the most basic and useful functions on the ALU. It is possible to design a simple version using a few connected transistors to simply add 1 byte of information to a secondary byte. This circuit is called a 1 bit adder and can be used to explain a few of the processes which allow a computer to add two numbers together. The diagram below shows how a set of transistors could be connected in a circuit to perform the calculation. As can be seen, there are two inputs A and B, both are connected as a voltage source 1 or 0. Depending on the combination of logic the outcome would be seen as an output in the connection of Sum. If the value is more than 1 byte there will also be an output in Cout which is the carry byte meaning there was an overflow in the calculation. This is used when the binary exceeds the expected output. The circuit also has a live Vcc and ground as the circuit is designed to be simulated on a board.

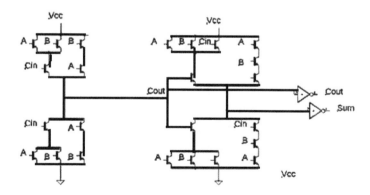

Fig 5.2.2 A 1 Byte adder created using transistors

To take this principle further the circuit can be extended to calculate more than one byte of information. Where the carry byte is used as an input to the secondary circuit. As can be seen from the picture below the circuit has more than two inputs as the binary will have 4 bits of input and contain 16 bytes (decimal) of information. Meaning that the circuit is able to perform a calculation up to the value of 16. This circuit forms the basis of the 4 bit adder.

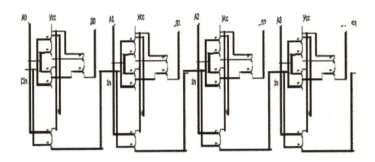

Fig 5.2.2 A 4 bit adder created using transistors

From the design of the transistor circuit it might not be possible to see the digital logic which exists on the circuit board. Each 1 bit adder is comprised of an OR gate into the first output and an AND gate which creates a secondary output or carry. This has the function of memorising if a value has occurred and carrying the secondary value to the next adder. This performs a ripple effect across the digital logic, until the whole calculation across each input has occurred. To explain the circuit in more detail the network can be explained using logic gates which create the same process. Below is a diagram of the circuit using gates to replace the transistors.

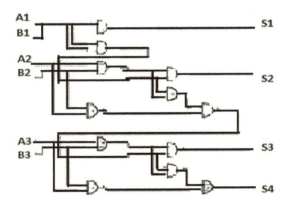

Fig 5.2.2 Logic gate explanation for 4 bit adder

The logic gates for the circuit might allow a better explanation as it is easier to describe the principles which allow the circuit to work. As can be seen the SR latch creates a binary state in the output and the AND and OR gates allow the circuit to logically determine the calculation. The SR latch stores the current output once the calculation has been completed. Obviously, depending on the size of the ALU the circuit will have more than 4 bytes. Most computers are in the range of 32 to 64 bytes meaning that they are able to perform very complex calculations, and number ranges.

5.2.3 Creating a subtract module using two's complement

The two's complement method of subtraction allows one number in binary to be converted to a minus value before being added to a secondary number. How this works is that the minus number is greater than the ordinary value, so that when the two are added the increment sends the two values into a secondary cycle. To achieve this a value is made negative by inverting all the values in the register. For instance -5 can be processed using the following formula.

```
 5 =  00000101
      11111010    complement digits
           +1     add 1
-5 =  11111011
```

The diagram below shows how this circuit might be designed in an ALU. The inverted circuitry is attached to the adding module which creates a logical output from the two input registers.

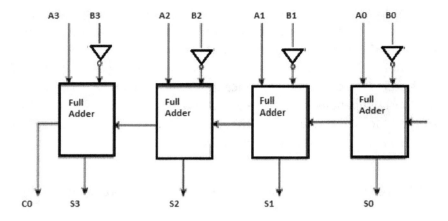

Fig 5.2.3 Circuit of a subtraction module in an ALU

5.2.4 Increment and decrement using the shift register

The shift register is another example of a part of the ALU which functions to perform calculations to data which is stored on the register. Again the shift register is designed separately to other parts of the system, but is connected via a data bus to allow the component to access the register. Once the component is activated the shift register will either increment or decrement 1 byte of binary to the data contained on the bus. This is completed every clock cycle. For instance one pulse to the clock element will add 1 byte of binary the second pulse will add another byte, incrementing the data. The diagram below describes how this circuit is connected as a set of digital gates.

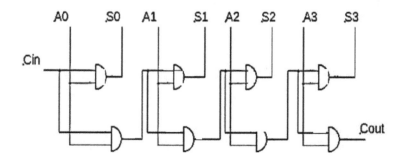

Fig 5.2.4 an incrementing shift register seen as logic gates

The circuit is designed a lot like the digital adder, except there is only one set of inputs for one register, and a clock timer which creates the inputs through the latches. This would work in tandem with the accumulator to repeatedly store the incrementing binary data. Incrementing data is not the only function which the shift register is able to achieve. The component also provides the function of decrementing the data as well. This time the clock pulse will reduce the binary by 1 byte with every signal. During a program the shift register will allow a number to reduce to zero, before moving to the next routine. In fact it is possible to use this function in a number of ways. The diagram below describes how this function is achieved using logic gates.

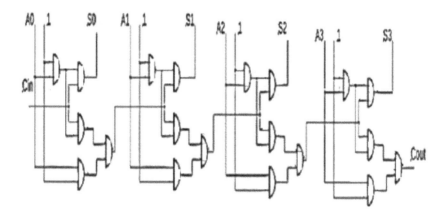

Fig 5.2.4 logic gates for a decrementing shift register

The circuit takes the information from the data bus and uses a series of gates to manipulate the binary in the register. This can again be seen in the second picture which provides the same circuits, in transistors as they might appear on a chip or arithmetic board.

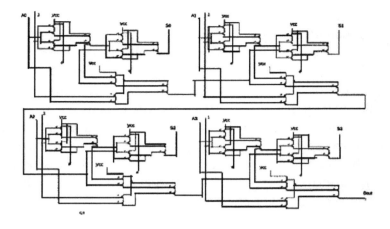

Fig 5.2.4 Transistor circuit for a decrementing shift register

5.3.1 Logic and comparison functions

The arithmetical functions of the computer are not the only processes the ALU carries out. The increment and addition functions are completed by only part of the ALU. There is also a separate unit which deals with the comparisons and logical functions. These are two processes which are completed using similar circuitry to perform the procedures; and are contained in a different part of the ALU. The logic unit is accessed on the data bus using the same address pathway as the arithmetic unit as both exist on the same system. To understand the processes which the comparison unit carries out it is necessary to identify some of the functions. The table below describes some of the processes conducted by this module.

TYPES OF LOGIC AND COMPARISON FUNCTIONS	
AND	Less than
OR	Greater than
NOT	Equals to
XOR	Byte compare

Table 5.3.1 Types of functions completed by the logic unit

As can be seen logical functions act a lot like logic gates except that the data which is passed can be more than one byte. The comparison functions are slightly different, as these types of instructions simply provide a carry flag if two numbers are identical or different. For instance a computer program might jump to a new instruction if two values are the same. This could be completed by a carry flag being set if each byte on the register are identical to the output signals sent to the AND gates. Other compare functions could also be completed by subtracting one value form another and carry flag being set if a negative value is achieved meaning that the value had been less than. The comparison unit needs to provide these types of instructions.

A computer program will usually use one these types of commands when the code needs to test parameters. For instance a number of jump sequences are used in conditional programming depending on the analysis of data sets. This can be done through using either logic functions or comparisons. The unit simply provides a carry flag which changes the condition of the stack pointer. For example an instruction could push the memory address onto the stack and the next instruction only pushes the stack if the carry flag has been set. These types of sequences allow computer programs to be dynamic and multidimensional.

5.3.2 Designing a comparison function

To better understand the comparison unit the diagram below is a simple design of a bit compare function in an ALU. The unit is used to take two binary numbers from a register and test each byte using a series of logical AND gates. The unit itself can test either all or a single byte between the two registers. This is achieved by the AND gates setting a byte on the D Flip Flops of the accumulator if a Vcc source is detected from any one of the logic gates. The accumulator then uses a series of gates to create a bit set or carry flag which identifies when a condition has been met on the register. This flag is used to complete the next instruction which pushes the contents of the stack onto the address register, to jump to the next program. The accumulator can also store the result of any operation.

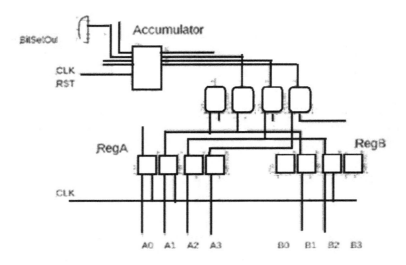

Fig 5.3.2 design of a simple comparison function

This is a simple design for a bit compare on an ALU. There are many more types of functions which can be made using similar processes depending on the design of the computer. Again it is worth pointing out that many conditions can be made by running a function of a number of processes which lowers the instruction set needed. For instance a greater than function can be completed by using the subtract and compare commands; which provides the same outcome.

End of Chapter Quiz

Why types of functions do ALU unit complete?

Draw a block diagram of an ALU unit?

When are ALU instructions used in a program?

Identify a type of circuit used in an ALU?

6

Mathematical Procedures

In this chapter you will look at the following

- Identify procedures which use the ALU
- The ALU block diagram
- Opcodes and addressing modes
- Using the ALU to create a procedure

6.1.1 How does the computer use the ALU?

The last chapter identified the structures which exist in the ALU. The module itself is considered to be primarily based around mathematical processes, and is able to mimic basic formulas which are used to complete a mathematical task. For this reason the ALU is usually designed around basic calculation type instructions such as add, subtract and multiply. These instructions from the basis of the procedures used inside spreadsheets and certain database type software. The ALU is also used for other types of queries as it is often used by the CPU to complete ordinary tasks during the run time of a program. The CPU requires the logic unit to process various types of instructions. Where the CPU has to respond to ordinary tasks which involve data manipulation or logic. For this reason it useful to understand that the ALU is not only used for arithmetic but for processing and coding instructions.

6.1.2 Procedures which use the ALU

To develop the concept of how the computer uses the ALU it is necessary to identify a number of procedures which use the ALU during a program execution or runtime. The obvious place to start is a small program which uses the structures in the ALU to create a squared value from an ordinary number. The ALU itself does not actually have a command which is able to complete this process. However it is possible to use the processes which exist in the ALU using a different format. The program could be easily achieved on most systems if the CPU had the ability to add two values together and also decrement the registers. The following code describes how the query could be written using assembly language to complete the process.

```
Mov a, 22              //Move value to a register
Mov b, 22              //mov identical value into other register

RunSquared
Add, a, 22
Dec b                  //add value in registers and decrement b
Call RunSquared
DJNZ                   // Repeat process and jump when zero
Print acc,             //Print the result stored in the accumulator
```

The way this procedures works is quite simple as it is asking the computer to find the squared number of a value through the use of multiplication. As a mathematical process the squared value of a number is the number multiplied by itself.

Square = n *n   or
484 = 22 * 22

The computer might not be actually be able to complete this process using these commands as the CPU might on occasion not have a multiplication function. Or the software does not use multiplication. For either reason the code has to be written in a way which the computer can identify with. This problem can be seen in the code which is able to complete the process yet works in slightly different way than is expected. How the program works is by adding the value to itself 22 times. Which is seen as a multiplication type function. The code adds 22 to the value and continues to repeat until the value in B reaches 0 and the program jumps to the print instruction. This then prints the result of 22 squared which solves the equation. This would represent how the ALU is used to manipulate types of mathematical procedures.

There are other processes which need to use the ALU to complete the procedures. For instance the logic unit might be needed to coordinate the conditional events which occur during a program. A command might also need to add the value of two numbers to work out the location of a memory address. Such as the use of data tables. For this reason the ALU can be used to function above mathematical procedures and coordinate events inside the CPU. The following example is using the carry flag to move different parts of a program.

Pint favourite mode of transport

```
Routine 1
Ld string 255, a          //load string value from location 255 "how do
                             you like to travel"
Print a
Ld a Input                //Load value in keyboard input
Comp a, 560               //compare binary value "car" in location 560
BTFSC                     //Skip next instruction if carry flag set
Call NotPreferred
Call Preferred

Preferred
Print string 340          //Print that is how I like to travel

NotPrefered
Print string 380          //I do not travel that way myself
```

This explains another function which is not typical to the commands of the ALUs structure but allows the program to create a conditional jump sequence to another routine depending on the input written in a computer key board. What the program is trying to do is ask 'how do you like to travel'. Depending on the response the computer will print the following.

''That is how I like to travel'   or
'I do not travel that way myself'

These responses are stored on two memory addresses 340 and 380. The computer uses the compare function to identify if the input from the user has the same value in binary as the value for car. The ALU uses the logical unit during the program to compare the two binary results. The compare sets a carry flag which then jumps to either memory location which contains the response.

6.2.1 Understanding typical addressing modes in an ALU

An addressing mode is simple the way in which an instruction is decoded by the control unit, and processed by the relevant part of the computer. The ALU is obviously a separate component to others which exist on the processor unit, and has its own set of instructions which have access to the different structures within the system. For instance a computers commands or instructions will have a number of functions such as addition and subtraction which only access parts of the ALU. To make this simpler to complete, instructions are often grouped together so that similar instructions have similar coding in binary, for instance a group of instruction might be listed as follows for different commands.

0001 – 1FFF = Arithmetic functions
2000 – 2FFF = Graphics
3000 – 3FFF = Sound
4000 – 4FFF= Strings
5000 – 5FFF = Loops
6000 – 6FFF = data tables

This means that the opcode for an arithmetic instruction on a 16 byte system, would be somewhere between 0001 and 1FFF. Any instruction in binary between these two points would be used by the ALU. The amount of real instruction might actually be limited to fewer commands than that which is available in terms of space. This is because each instruction might have a number of addressing sequences which changes the context of how each instruction is used. For instance an addition instruction might be coded in a number of formats which determines which register it is reading during the procedure. This type of indexed addressing is common to most types of instructions as they are often listed as containing variations in use.

For the purpose of the text we are only going to look at addressing modes used within the ALU to determine if the process is going to be an arithmetical or logic function. To understand this process the diagram below depicts the separate modules within the ALU. As can be seen the two modules need their own binary code to be activated. Which determines the function which is being selected from the unit.

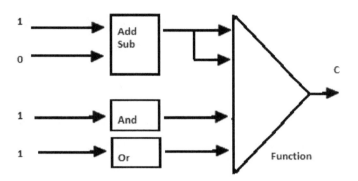

Fig 6.2.1 MUX design for arithmetic addressing

For instance

1000 = Addition
1001 = Subtraction

0100 = AND
0101 = OR

Here the first two bytes of code represent which module is being used. The second two bytes refer to which type of function is being selected. Obviously if there is a large instruction set there will be a greater number of instruction references. For the purpose of explaining the decoder it is only necessary to use four instructions. Although this application could be used within larger scale designs which use a greater number of instruction references. The instructions used above have two modules representing the logical and arithmetical functions. The purpose is to separate the logical structure of the unit and allow the commands to select the correct instruction. This process works alongside the control unit to determine which instruction is being carried out and what part of the computer has access to overall processes such as the address bus and data bus.

During the design of a computers modules it is necessary to determine how each unit will have an addressing mode per instruction and also the types of indexed addressing which exist per module. The reason is that the overall design and complexity of the computer is determined by these processes. The use of appropriate coding also determines how the program structures will be completed during a routine. Identifying these types of processes are important considerations, as the processor is only able to respond to each instruction as it is read.

6.3.1 Opcode and operand of mathematical instruction

As described earlier instructions are usually sent to the CPU's decoder in two parts. The first part would normally be the operation the instruction is due to perform and the second part is a chunk of data which the instruction refers to. For instance if we use the addition function from the MUX which was designed earlier, we could design a method of writing the instruction which allows the data to be used within a program.

Opcode	Operand	ASM code	Meaning
1000	1010	Add #10	Add 10 to current procedure

It is possible to take this instruction further and turn the procedure onto a small program which adds two numbers and stores the result in memory location 15.

0100 1000	Ld #10	//Ld 10 into the accumulator
1000 0011	Add #3	//add 3 to the accumulator
0111 1111	STA 15	//store the result in location 15

The program itself is quite simple as it merely adds two numbers together. But it describes a set of instructions which are based on the premise of using an opcode and operand. This method of sending data is preferred as it allows the decoder space to interpret a data signal or instruction. Basically the bandwidth is merely split in two. This allows some instructions to have no operand or others to only contain data. This is not the only method of sending data as there are addressing techniques which allow certain instructions to be sent to different parts of the CPU. Consider another instruction which as more than 4 bytes for the opcode.

```
01100110 00000000 Mov A, b    //Move the contents of a to reg b
10001000 00001010 Add B,10    //Add 10 to reg b
```

These instructions appear to be quite similar yet they use a larger bandwidth to describe the opcode. For instance the second instruction is still used to add 10 to the register, but this time it describes which register to add the number to. This would be achieved through using the bytes directly after the mathematical instruction. This is another method of addressing. The principle is that one instruction can be decoded to perform a number of sequences depending on the part of the instruction which is used to describe the addressing mode. It is actually quite simple to interpret what type for addressing is being used by looking at how the asm code is written. For example

```
Add 10, a      //add 10 to register
Add a, b       //addition between registers – store in a
Add a, 255     // add the contents of 255 to reg a
Add 63, a      // Add value 63 to a
```

All of these values are used for the purpose of addition except each method describes a different type of addressing mode to achieve the same purpose. On limited computers a set of instructions, might only move data around the register in one way. Whereas on more complex computers data can be moved throughout the CPU in a number of ways. This allows tasks to be completed in a number of methods which increase the variety and complexity of the design. For instance small computers might be only be able to add a value to the contents of an accumulator, which could achieve a limited number of programs. Whereas larger data manipulation would require a number of techniques to locate and move the current data instructions.

TYPES OF ADDRESSING MODES

IMMEDIATE	Register indirect
DIRECT	Based
REGISTER	Implied
INDEXED	

Table 6.3.1 Types of functions completed by the logic unit

6.3.2 Mathematical instruction functions

To create any type of function or procedure it is necessary to have a clear understanding of what the procedure is trying to achieve. This applies to writing code for the application of mathematical functions. Due to most CPU's having only a few instructions for the purpose of arithmetic, it is often necessary to write more complex procedures called lambda equations, which are able to use the small instruction to complete more complex tasks like percentages. The key to understanding this process is developing the code in short hand, which details the actual equation, before committing this to a number of processes. The following example explains how to complete a simple percentage formula.

Percentage equation
Z = 25% 0f 87 = 21.75

This could be presented as the following code

```
Select number
Mov a, 87
Create percentage
Exp a, 100     //change the exponent of a
Mov b 25
Add a, acc
Dec b
Djnz           //jump when reaches zero
Return
```

Here the code can be done in a number of ways as there are many types of formulas which handle the mathematical expressions for finding a percentage. The code here relies on the processors ability to use a floating-point number. How a floating-point number works is by taking a value and changing the exponent of that value. The code moves the decimal place so that the whole number becomes a fraction. This is then multiplied by the value of percent until the answer has been obtained. This example describes how to convert a formula in shorthand and create a procedure which obtains the solution to the function. Many types of formulas are able to be solved in the same way using limited bandwidth of instruction sets.

6.4.1 Floating point numbers and status registers

Binary numbers do not act the same way as a decimal number as the values are obtained in a different format which effects the way they behave in formulas. To be able to use fractions on the ALU a system has been created which moves the value into two parts. For example

Decimal	Exponent	Mantissa
87.3=	0101 0111	0000 0011

Here the exponent and the mantissa have to be coded as two separate numbers. For example during a percentage equation. 87 is divided by 100 and so is the fraction. The code would then have to use both values to obtain the result.

6.4.2 The status register

The final point to note regarding the ALU is the components interaction with the status register. Here the set of D flip flops create an output signal depending on response from the ALU's logic unit. For instance the status register will have a carry and minus flag as well as a number of conditions such overflow and zero. These are used within programs to determine if conditions which exist within the logic unit have occurred, as well as the events which happen in the accumulator during certain procedures. The status register determines if certain events might affect procedures and is used to prevent and describe errors.

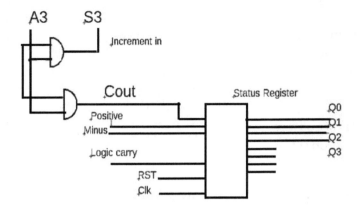

Fig 6.4.2 a circuit explaining a carry flag for a status register

The above diagram describes the process in which a binary number becomes too large for the shift register which creates a signal to the status flag,

End of Chapter Quiz

Is the ALU only used for arithmetic?

How are the instructions effected by addressing modes?

Design a MUX which determines the instruction

Identify a potential use of a lambda equation?

7

Fetch Decode Cycle

In this chapter you will look at the following

- Interpret the fetch decode cycle flow chart
- Determine the components used during the fetch cycle
- Identify how the stack and the program counter retrieve data
- Determine the events which occur during a program

7.1.1 What is the fetch decode cycle?

This process is important to understand as it underpins the events which occur each time an instruction or routine is called. There are also a number of important stages which occur during this procedure and is fundamental to how the computer is designed. The fetch decode cycle is actually a number of processes which determine how each instruction is decoded by the computer. The usual method of the cycle is to fetch the instruction from the memory, decode and perform the instruction before setting the program counter to the next event. These stages are controlled by a timer and control unit. They have to be completed in turn so that the data and instructions are able to be decoded by the correct part of the computer.

To better understand the fetch cycle, it is necessary to look at what occurs during a single instruction, and what takes place during the procedure across the CPU. Each action is not allowed to interfere with other processes. For this reason the fetch decode cycle creates a method of decoding an instruction before moving onto the next task. The cycle begins when the program counter calls the instruction and ends when the next instruction is called. The diagram below shows the stages which occur during a single cycle.

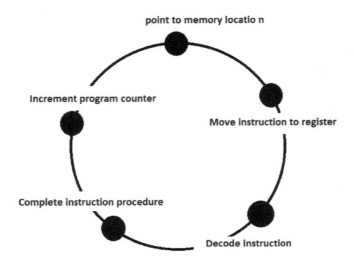

Fig 7.1.1 A diagram describing the fetch cycle

As can be seen the cycle runs through each stage and repeats the same process over again. This allows the computer to decode an instruction and complete all the processes which need to occur during each phase. Some instructions need to complete other tasks such as checking the status register. For this reason the fetch cycle has more stages than needed for every instruction, but this depends on the task being carried out.

7.1.2 The fetch decode cycle flow chart

During the fetch cycle an instruction is read and then decoded which means that the decoder needs to interact with a number of components including the program memory and ALU. This means that certain processes need to be controlled so that they do not interfere with other instruction being carried out. This is important as certain functions such as the data bus need to be timed between other processes and events. The diagram below shows a simple flow chart of an instruction being called from memory.

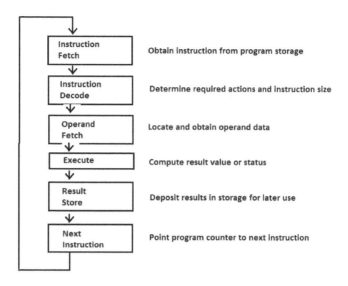

Fig 7.1.2 flow chart describing each phase

The explanation here is quite general and does not describe the interactions of each type of instruction. As can be seen the cycle begins when the program counter points to a new address or location in memory, this provides an instruction across the data bus, which is then moved to the instruction register or decoder. This register is actually part of the CPU so the data which is sent from memory is sent directly to the CPU. This instruction is then decoded and sent to the relevant part of the CPU, before being processed and incrementing the program counter to the next instruction located in the memory. This begins the process again, effectively incrementing the entire contents of memory until a change in the programs structure.

7.2.1 Understanding the components which complete the fetch cycle.

The fetch cycle represents how each event is timed and processed during a clock cycle. This sequence is actually completed by the control unit, which is the part of the CPU which dictates the timing of events. How this works is that the control unit will respond to the instruction held in memory and provide a set of responses which decide which component is being accessed across the data bus. This is completed by a number of clock cycles sending a signal source to the chip enable of each part in turn. This allows the chips to not access the data bus at the same time, which allows each process the time to work. The control unit has a number of decoded networks which read the addressing from the opcode, and responds by completing the appropriate set of commands. These events are timed against a clock, meaning the events will usually take place between T0-T5 meaning that each instruction completes 5 cycles to complete a process.

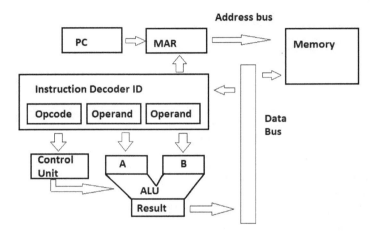

Fig 7.2.1 Diagram of the components needed during instruction cycle

7.2.2 The program counter

The cycle begins with the program counter pointing to the location in memory. This allows the instruction held in the current memory address to be read by instruction registers and held in the CPU. The PC is basically a shift register which increments each time a clock pulse is sent to the CLK input. This allows each memory address to be selected in turn each time it is incremented. The program counter also has a byte input allowing a memory address to be sent from the stack any time a call instruction occurs during a program. To understand the program counter in more detail, the diagram below shows the digital logic needed to complete the call and increment function. The clk pulse completes the increment process across the shift register and the Write/Enable allows the program counter to load input directly from the stack. The PC begins the instructions cycle.

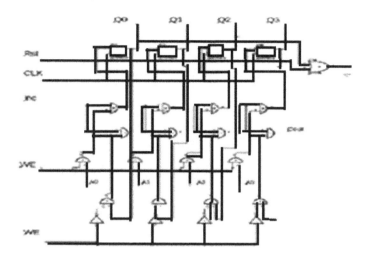

Fig 7.2.2 the digital decoder found in the program counter

The entire circuit for program counter can be found in fig 7.2.2. This describes the wiring needed to allow the program counter to directly call a memory address. Each byte of the program counter is read directly by the ROMs which locates the instruction according to which memory line it is pointing at.

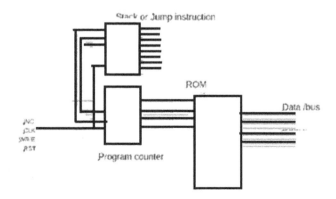

Fig 7.2.2 Wiring of the program counter for selecting a memory location

7.2.3 Decoding the opcode in the instruction register

During the procedure of decoding an instruction. The instruction held in memory is passed to the instruction register. This is a decoder which is attached to a shift register which is large enough to hold a single instruction. The register is connected to a number of decoders which read the instruction and process the information according to the purpose of the opcode. For instance an instruction might need to access the ALU or pass a parameter inside the stack register. The instruction decoder provides the correct addressing to allow the instruction to be completed. The decoder will also work out what type of instruction is being requested as some instructions have a number of different variations, according to the procedure. Depending on the result of the instruction the result will then be stored in the accumulator, or if accessing the memory retrieve the correct memory address.

PURPOSE OF THE FETCH DECODE CYLCE	
SEPERATE COMMANDS	Time events
CONTROL PROCESSES	Reduce errors
DECODE INSTRUCTIONS	

Table 7.2.3 Types of functions completed by the logic unit

Once the instruction has been completed and the program counter incremented, the fetch cycle has finished and repeats again with a new instruction. The CPU and memory perform most of the work needed to complete the process, this includes the control unit and instruction register. The table above explores why the CPU needs to read instructions in this way.

7.3.1 The clock timer

The control unit can be seen as the part of the CPU which performs the movements needed for the instruction to be processed. The control unit has a number of digital logic sequences which interprets the instruction pathways across the data bus. Effectively allowing the data to move across the circuitry. Each clock pulse across the cycle allows the instruction to move throughout the CPU. As mentioned earlier a fetch cycle would usually have between T0 and T5 stages. The clock pulse signifies the start of a new stage in the cycle, moving the pointer to a new process across the digital logic. The diagram below describes a simplified digital circuit which shows how the timer is connected to the various outputs through a series of logic gates.

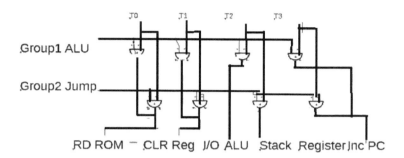

Fig 7.3.1 simplified control unit identifying the timer

As can be seen the timer is used to control the sequence of events which occur during each instruction. Every clock pulse provides a new signal source to the inputs, which allow the instruction to move across the various outputs. For instance the first clock pulse points to the read memory address, and ends when the program counter is incremented. The output which occurs between these points perform the functions needed for the instruction. These are specific to the instruction and the events dictate how the data bus is used and which parts of the CPU need to be connected. For instance, a command which needs the ALU, would need data to be moved across the CPU, whereas others might need access to the other outputs such as the visual processing unit. Here the timed sequences would interact with the addressing of the instruction and the input provided by the timer.

The timer itself is usually a shift register which provides an output to each part of the control unit in sequence. It is possible to make the timer from an oscillator and a number of flip flops joined in series. This would provide the expected sequence of outputs. The amount of stages used by the timer determine the length of the clock cycle and how long a process takes to complete. For instance it is possible to work out how long a program takes to complete by determining the amount of instructions needed to perform the routine and then multiplying this by the amount of phases in the control unit. This is useful when identifying how long a program takes to complete before it is possible to move onto the next procedure. For instance the formula below describes how to perform the calculation

Formula for clock speed:

Clock speed x number of instructions
Routine has 100 instruction 0.05 s/instruction = 5 seconds to perform routine

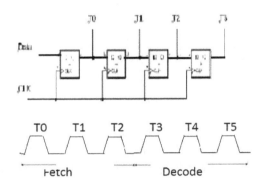

Fig 7.3.1 shift register used to create a clock sequence

The diagram above shows a simple shift register used to create the timing sequences inside the control unit. The speed of the oscillator determines the clock pulse.

7.4.1 Calling a simple procedure

To further explore how the fetch cycle works, it is necessary to consider a simple program procedure where a group of instructions are called from memory for the purpose of moving a number of ASCII codes to a keyboard output. The intention is to describe how each timer sequence moves the data across the computer. The code might be written as the following:

Mov a, 0000 0001
Output Print a,
Mov a, 0000 0010
Output Print a,
Mov a, 0000 0011
Output Print a,

Here there are two instructions which are repeated until a printout reads abc. The first instruction moves a binary value into the register which is decoded by a peripheral interface from the ASCII code equivalent for the letter a. The second instruction moves the data into the peripheral. Completing the routine. The actual movement of the data would occur in a number of stages as listed in the table below.

Clk	Process in cycle
T0	Read address in program counter
T1	Mov value from ROM to instruction register
T2	Check status flags
T3	Mov binary to register a
T4	Increment program counter

As can be seen the data needs to move a value which occurs in a series of five stages. Each stage uses a different part of the computer in sequence. For instance the first stage needs to interact with the program counter and memory to locate the instruction. The second stage needs to move the binary form the memory location across the data bus, before being decoded by the CPU. What occurs during each stage of the process is the control unit allowing one component to work before moving to the next component. The table below shows the events which occur during the next instruction.

Clk	Process in cycle
T0	Read address in program counter
T1	Mov value from ROM to instruction register
T2	Mov register a to peripheral
T3	Output value in peripheral
T4	Increment program counter

The Print instruction shares a number of the same routines. The instruction still reads from the program memory before moving the contents to the CPU. The difference is that the instruction uses a peripheral connection to create a keyboard output. The process is again coordinated by the control unit which uses a timer sequence to select the correct part of the CPU. The entire process is completed in a series of stages, where the clock counter and the chip enable (C/E) of each component allows the expected output to occur. The entire process creates the one event inside the program, yet happens within 5 timed responses, completed by the control unit. The diagram below shows the movement across the computers CPU.

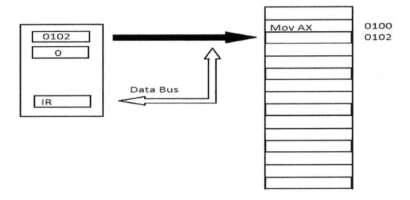

Fig 7.4.1 Flow chart for decoding an instruction

What occurs during this simple procedure is the movement of the data across the data bus, into the relevant pathways. The idea is that the instructions are listed inside the ROM of the computer and selected in turn. The instruction is then sent to the relevant registers which allow the instruction to be read and decoded. The fetch cycle illustrates how the data moves between each part. Due to the format in which the computer responds to different timed sequences. Each instruction needs to follow the same procedure each time it is called. The component which is selected during the instruction, depends on the addressing of the opcode and the intended function. The fetch decode cycle relies on most of the components on the board to work, meaning that the control unit has to do a lot of work to coordinate the various signals.

7.5.1 The read/write cycle

It is worth pointing out how a chip uses the pathways on the data and address bus. As the information which is sent across these parts of the computer interacts with a number of different sets of chips. For instance it was seen how the address bus is used to select the current memory location, which communicates with a number of systems including the stack and program counter. The data bus acts in a similar way as the ports are usually I/O meaning that they are both input and output across the bus. Information which is sent on the bus between the memory and outputs etc, sometime interact with the chip sets in different ways. The CPU needs to receive the data bytes as well as move them along to other parts. Again this process is coordinated through the use of the control unit. This part of the CPU decides whether an input is either read or write, and sets the data path into the relevant cycle. The diagram below shows a simple chips interface detailing the inputs needed to change how the information is perceived on the data bus.

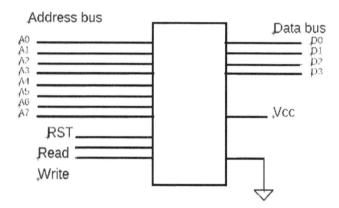

Fig 7.5.1 read/write interface of memory chip

As can be seen form the diagram the ROM is connected to a data bus which is used to move the instruction. The port which is connected to the data bus is I/O meaning that information across the bus can be either sent or received. The way this is achieved is through applying a voltage signal to the read I/O input. The chip is designed to have a number of inputs which determine if the state of the port is in either read or write.

The circuitry inside the chip determines what status the chip is currently being used in. For instance during a usual program procedure the data bus will be in a write status, whereas when a program is being committed to memory the chips status will be designated as read. Meaning that the chip will be storing any information which is on the data bus. Again the control unit controls this process as part of an instruction's procedure which will include what status certain components are working under. Which allows each instruction to move across the CPU.

Allowing the chips to work in this way is important to the overall movement of data, as it is possible to compress the data bus into one system. Using this method means that data has access to all the chips connected across the system. The only problem is interfacing the chip to the control unit, as the data bus cannot provide the access to the chip enable pins. This is achieved instead via small circuitry attached to the instruction decoder and control unit, which is carried across by the control bus. For instance a calculation instruction will determine whether it is logical or arithmetic as well as the component itself. The information found to decide this is held within the addressing part of the opcode. The next chapter will discuss how addressing methods are selected in the control unit to determine the status of components as they are used.

End of Chapter Quiz

What is the purpose of the fetch decode cycle?

Identify a number of components which are used in the process?

Design a simple control unit timer procedure?

Draw the W/R inputs to a memory device across the data bus?

Control Unit Stages and Interfacing

In this chapter you will look at the following

- An explanation of a control unit
- Format for addressing instructions
- Interfacing the control unit
- Designing a simple module

8.1.1 An overview of the purpose of a control unit?

The last chapter explained what occurs during a fetch decode cycle. The decode cycle describes the processes which are completed during the decoding of an instruction. The main component of this procedure is the control unit. The control unit contains the circuitry and timing mechanisms needed to move the instruction across the CPU and data bus. Once an instruction is decoded within the instruction register, it passes the information to the control unit. Without this component the information contained on the instruction would be unable to move beyond the systems memory. The picture below describes the basic flow of information from the module. As can be seen the unit is responsible for interpreting the information from the instruction registers, and using the data to interact with the interfaced components across the control bus.

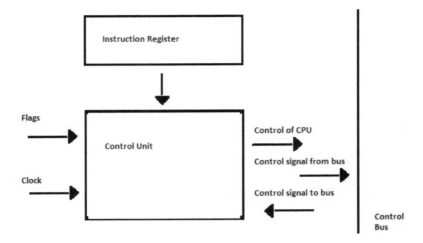

Fig 8.1.1 Basic flow of information to the control unit

8.1.2 Basic design of a control unit

The control unit is designed around a number of processes. The timer inside the unit is used to time the sequence in which an instruction is moved around the computers structure. The timer interacts with information from the instruction a lot like a MUX which is able to control the sequences of outputs from just the one instruction. For instance the LDA instruction will interact with the signal from the timer between T0 and T5 allowing the instruction to move across the control bus. This is completed through the use of a number of circuits and digital logic gates which are able to manipulate the pathway of the information coming from the instructions binary data. This is mainly achieved through the addressing references designated to a particular instruction. For instance certain instructions share similar binary data as they directly interact with the same components.

The diagram below provides a block diagram of how the components are interfaced so that they are able to interact with the instruction register and control bus. The diagram shows how the inputs are relevant to a number of instructions and also how the inputs from the ring counter are able to be used to create a matrix of outputs from the control unit, by timing this with each instruction.

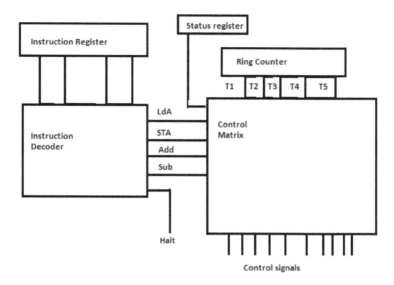

Fig 8.1.2 simple interface for a control unit

8.2.1 Instruction addressing and the format used by the control unit

Addressing modes relate to how the instruction is decoded and how the CPU responds to the information provided by the instruction. For instance a single instruction might have a number of variations which mean that the instruction can be used to complete a number of different sequences. An example of this can be found in the ALU as this component has a number of methods of storing the product of a result once a calculation has been completed. The instruction below describes a number of uses of a single function for addition.

Add a, 255
Store accumulator
Store in memory address
Read from memory address
Mov to register

As can be seen the instruction is used to add 255 to the register a. although it is possible to achieve this in a number of ways. Here the product can be stored in the accumulator or moved to a memory address and stored in the RAM. Many types of instructions behave in a similar way where the instruction can be manipulated so that the single instruction has a number of separate methods. This is achieved by the computer by a form of addressing or pathways which reads the binary form the opcode and interprets the instruction according to the information presented. This is usually achieved through the use of a MUX or a matrix of connections which identify the opcode and provide the necessary response. Addressing modes allow for more dynamic program structures and also less complicated networks of circuits.

8.2.2 Creating an instruction set for a module

Consider the module below which is for the design of a simple 4 bit CPU. The module is used for arithmetic but also has a series of I/O ports which allow the data to connect to a peripheral device. Due to the way some of the processes complete the same procedure, it is possible to group the instructions into a number of sets. For each group of commands the timing procedure will work in exactly the same way. For instance, during a calculation the control bus merely manipulates access to the ALU. For this reason any group of instructions which use the same component can be grouped into the same instruction reference or procedure.

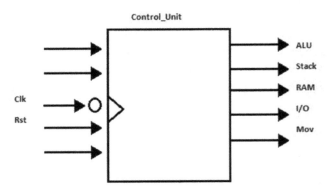

Fig 8.2.2 diagram of a simple control unit

The list below shows how many groups of instructions actually exist across the 4 bit CPU.

Stack function and call parameter
ALU arithmetic and logic unit
I/O ports and peripheral control
Load and move information

The 4 bit binary code can now be rewritten into a new format which allows the instruction to be grouped into each relevant type of procedure. This then allows the control unit to accurately move the information across the computer. This provides the following set of data forms, which group the functions into small chunks of binary. As there are 16 possible instructions it is possible to group the data set in to four groups of four. For instance.

0001-0100 = ALU commands
0101-1000 = Call commands
1001-1011= I/O commands
1100-1111 = Load and move commands

The digital logic for the binary can be seen in the diagram below. This allows each group of instructions to connect with the control bus and create a separate wiring system for each control qroup. The not values for the logic have been used as this reduced the overall dimensions of the circuit.

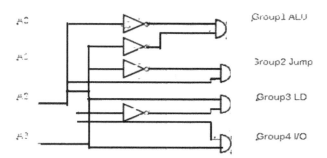

Fig 8.2.2 digital logic used to group procedures together.

TYPICAL CODING SETS OR GROUPS	
ARITHEMTIC	Peripheral
LOGICAL	Load
JUMP SEQUENCES	Visual
SOUND	

Table 8.2.2 Types of process that can be reduced to a group

8.2.3 More complex data formats

In more complex processes the control bus might need to complete more ranges of addressing modes, depending on the design of the system. For instance today's computers use a greater range of addressing modes which interact with procedures such as storage and ranges of registers where data is able to be held. Again the circuit needed to create these functions can be reduced to minimise the overall design and allow the computer to improve the performance of each function. Consider the diagram below which adds a separate MUX which determines if a code is being stored in the register or memory after being calculated. The control bus can be expanded to allow a simple function to be added to every instruction which is available on the control boards. Again when considering this type of option on a computer board it is necessary to look at how to minimise how many circuits this type of instruction might require.

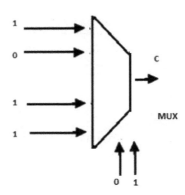

Fig 8.2.3 schematic of a MUX used for prioritising types of addressing

8.3.1 Identifying the instruction register

The purpose of the instruction decoder is to identify the instruction and provide the information to allow the computer to perform the routine. For instance an instruction which requires access to an I/O is relatively simple as the port only needs to be in a state of read or write. Some instructions are more important as they need to identify other processes such as interrupts and information held on the status register. This procedure is completed within the decoder and control unit. Again using the example from earlier it is possible to design a simple instruction decoder which allows each instruction to be decoded into a single output. This can be used in turn with the grouped function to design a circuit which completes the status checks and performs a routine.

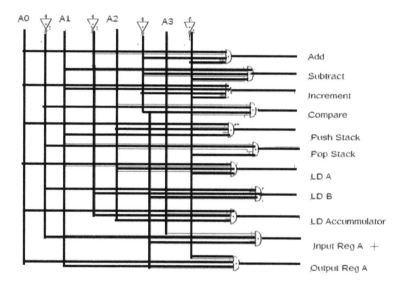

Fig 8.3.1 decoder used in an instruction register

Here the instructions are for a 4 bit CPU. Inside a larger system the control bus might complete the processes used to identify the instruction set and addressing. As well as contain a separate register which identifies certain procedure-based interrupts.

8.3.2 Timing in the control unit

The timing procedure is an important part of the fetch decode cycle, as it creates the stages an instruction works though when instruction passes through the computers CPU. The timing mechanism is the part of the computer which uses the control bus to switch each component on in turn, so that processes and events do not interfere with others. To complete this the control unit is wired into a ring counter which allows the timing module to sort through the logical gates according to the pathway of the individual instruction. The diagram below describes this process using the same CPU for the 4 bit system which was identified earlier. The process has been minimised by grouping the instructions to individual processes. As can be seen from the diagram all of the instruction begin by reading from the location in ROM, clearing the current register and incrementing the program counter. All of the commands include this process, as this part is used to read from memory.

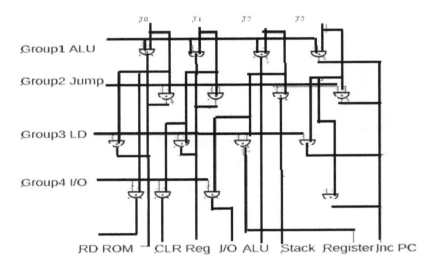

Fig 8.3.2 timing of a control unit

The rest of the procedures are specific to the current task and have a separate pathway to the control bus to complete these commands. It is worth mentioning that the control unit also has a number of conditional sequences such as the stack, which need to read the contents from the overflow and status registers, before being able to complete the instruction. This is due to the instruction needing to identify if a condition has been met. This can be achieved by using a separate register such as a d Flip flop which is able store a single byte of information to identify certain parameters in a program are correct. The diagram describes rewiring a standard register to use for the purpose of an interrupt signal.

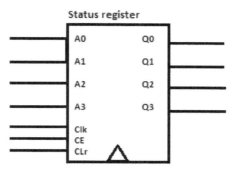

Fig 8.3.2 a simplified status register

8.4.1 The interfacing conditional commands

The control unit like the arithmetic module is based inside the CPU, meaning that it has direct access to certain functions such as the current instruction. When an instruction is being decoded this means that it usually has access to one set of responses across the control bus. The decoder determines how the instructions are then processed. Depending on the purpose of each instructions diagram the figure below describes the basic set of inputs and outputs which are used by the control unit. Interfacing conditional commands means adding an MUX which is able to infer further alternative outcomes depending on the instruction. For instance a decoder can be added to the control unit to manipulate the storage of data after calculations. This is usually referred to as addressing as it determines the register or memory location of the resultant calculation.

The instruction decoder in the diagram can be seen to consist of two parts. For instance one part of the instruction is directly relevant to aspects of the control bus which relate to the set or group the instruction belongs to. A further range of addressing allows a MUX to decide on further aspects of coding such as the location of the instructions result as well as deciding on the information found with the status register. These processes allow the overall dimensions of the control unit to be reduced, by limiting the number of logical gates which are required for the process to work. This also means that the instruction itself is coded in such a way that the instruction is split between its intended purpose and the mode in which it works. Which can be considered as a dimension of hard coding.

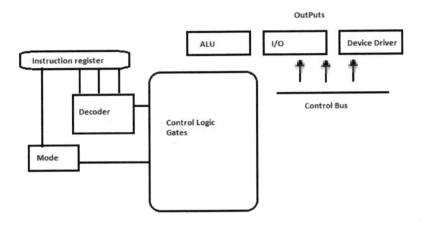

Fig 8.4.1 CPU interface of the control unit

End of Chapter Quiz

What does the control bus interact with?

Identify the interfaces of the control unit?

Describe process used to reduce the circuitry?

Design a binary instruction with more than one set of addressing?

Input Output Systems

In this chapter you will look at the following

- Identify the meaning of an I/O system
- The interface for an I/O device
- Explain device procedures such as coding and interrupts
- Design an encoder for an I/O

9.1.1 What is an I/O system?

Computers have I/O connections as it allows the system to be integrated with other devices allowing applications more versatility of use. A computer will usually contain a range of systems with which it is able to connect to for the sake of using various programmable utilities. For instance word uses a connection to a printer so that it is able to use the I/O connections to print readable documents. The expansion port or I/O is simply an interface which allows the peripheral to connect directly to the computer's internal system. For instance some applications such as keyboards are designed to move data into the system which the computers CPU can then manipulate. Due to the communication between devices usually being sent in binary, most interfaces are connected to some form of encoder for interpreting the information, as well as interfaces which allow the system to perform operations without interfering with other processes.

TYPES OF PERIPHERAL DEVICES

KEYOARD/ MOUSE	Speakers
PRINTER	Magnetic disk
EXPANDABLE MEMORY	USB
DISPLAY	

Table 9.1.1. Types I/O devices

The term I/O refers to the part of the computer which allows data to move information between devices. The interface for the system, generally has a number of ports which are able to be programmed to send and receive information across the computers data bus. The purpose of the I/O is to allow the system to perform tasks which connect to other devices such as keyboards and printers. The terminals located on the peripheral allow the data to travel across the bus and be stored in memory or used to manipulate programs. During communication the peripheral is able to directly access the terminal. Although there are still a set of procedures which the component needs to respond to for it to be able to complete the tasks. The status register on the chip's terminal determines which port is being used and what type of function is currently being conducted.

The method of successful communication between devices is achieved through applications or programs called device drivers, which are able to establish the correct methods of forming patterns and interrupts between the devices. For instance a computers scanner might need to request information from the program during downloads, as the information needs to be incorporated into the correct process. Without a means of communicating between protocols it would not be possible to create an accurate exchange of information. To achieve this the ports which are used to contain the I/O interface are connected to a number of integrated chips, which delegates how the information is sent across the ports. These work by containing a number of registers which are used to store the current status of the ports. For instance the chip decides whether the port is incoming or outgoing, as well as processing the interrupt requests during data connections. The diagram below identifies a number of systems all connected across the I/O system of a computer.

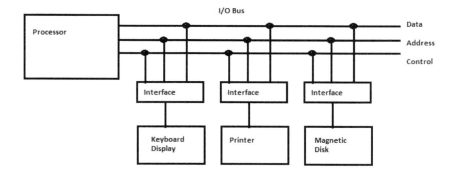

9.1.1 a typical connection across an I/O interface

As can be seen it is possible to have a number of connections across the I/O interface which all need access to the bus during the run time of a program or procedure. To achieve this a number of procedures are used which allows the program to dictate how the I/O port is currently being used.

9.1.2 Movement of data during communications

Any device connected to the systems hardware will need to be able to communicate in such a way that other systems are not affected. To achieve this the hardware is only able to be sent across the device when it is requested during a program. This is due to how information is processed by the computer. For instance the hardware connected to the port will only be able to send information when the program changes the conditions located on the ports control or status register. This will occur during a program, when certain conditions require information to be received and processed. The diagram below details the movement of data across the bus. The CPU communicates with the registers to demine the control of the data bus. The information is also sent across a number of buffers to allow data to not deteriorate while being sent. During communications the CPU will also be responsible for completing program procedures and responding to other tasks.

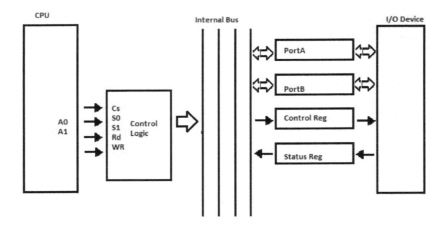

Fig 9.1.2 Movement of data during device procedures

The connections to the bus are similar to other processes such as the memory and display as the ports have their own address locations, this allows the procedures to interact directly with this part of the computer. For instance A8-A15 may only be for information sent to the CPU while data sent to addresses A0- A7 would go directly to the ports during a programme. Allowing a programme to directly access a port during a procedure as the information does not have to travel across the CPU during this process.

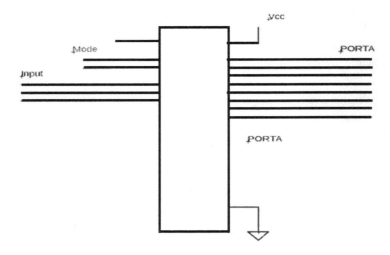

9.1.2 Wiring diagram of I/O port

9.2.1 The interface used on an I/O device

Despite modern wireless connections. The interface for a port would usually be a data connection across the bus, sent in either a parallel or serial connection. The connections to the ports would be shared with a series of chips which are programmed to determine how information is being requested and sent. To achieve this there are a number of status registers located in the chip which are able to store a binary state which identifies if the port is in either input or output mode. This component is used to identify if multiple devices are connected as well as identifying requests for information from devices during certain procedures. The status of the control register defines what procedure the port is committed to and how the port is intended to work. For instance during some processes the register is used to identify interrupts and schedule tasks between ports.

The interface for the ports are actually quite simple to create, as the port is merely a series of buffers which work independently of each other depending on which port is being selected. For instance there might be 3 ports on a terminal such as PORTS A, B, C each with its own connection. The ports would all share the same connection to the data bus, which is dependent on the current state of the status register. Effectively the state of the register determines which device has access to the board. The interface controls which port is being used and determines the interrupt sequence for other services which need access to the bus. When a data transfer is in process a series of protocols are used to decide whether information is being sent to or from the computer. This would usually be identified as a series of flags which changes the status of the port.

During a procedure the program will check to identify if a flag has been set in the status register before beginning a download. This procedure allows the component to check if the device is ready to begin a data connection and then prepares the data bus before loading the file. The port is able to complete a number of procedures dependent on the device. For instance some procedures require a number of interrupts for a program to work, such as touch typing, which allows the program to complete but periodically waits for other processes to occur such as data entry. This process is called polling which checks the port throughout a program to determine if a keypress has been met for example. This kind of event occurs when changing parameters inside a software procedure.

By changing the status of the control register, the circuit is able to work in a different format.

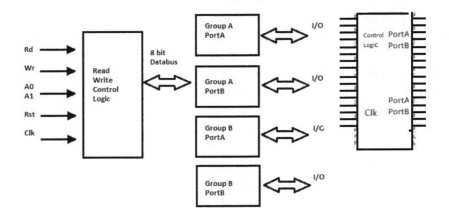

Fig 9.2.1 Layout of the I/O interface

9.3.1 Methods for creating device procedures.

As mentioned, communication across the ports often interferes with other procedures. For this reason the status register is used to establish which port or component has access to the data bus at any one time. This allows a program the functionality of the whole system without interfering with other processes. To improve this a set of communication protocols have been established. This method of data transfer is used in a variety of contexts such as WLAN for the internet and printer devices and even connecting a computer to an interface such as an LCD or segment display. By adhering to the same procedure a greater number of applications are able to be connected across the ports. Effectively the standard of data transfer creates an effective method of transferring data and files.

9.3.2 Different types of interrupt procedures

There are three main processes for data transfer across the ports. The most common type of process used to control devices during communication is the basic interrupt system. The interrupt pattern works by requesting the status of the control bus before transfer. Each part of a procedure is performed before allowing the next part to occur. This allows a programme to respond in stages which does not allow other events to occur. Creating an interrupt process is quite straight forward it simply requires the programmer to initiate a wait command before obtaining access to the data bus. This is an effective form of communication between devices but is inappropriate where number of systems need access the data bus. A more modern method uses the programmable interrupt which is able to handle a number of devices at the same time, where each use their own procedures. This allows priority over certain events.

The final method of communication transfer is the (DMA) or direct memory access. This is used in advanced systems which need to transfer huge amounts of data. The DMA system is used in USB types and is wired directly into the board. The component is able to establish a connection directly to the memory without needing to correspond with the CPU. This allows information to be saved onto memory without the need to run chunks of request patterns. Removing wait times and able to use larger formatted data files.

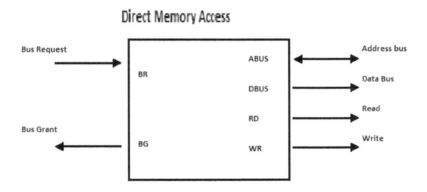

Fig 9.3.2 chip design for a direct memory access controller

9.4.1 Connecting a peripheral to the system

Due to how the system transfers data it is possible to connect a port to other devices other than common forms such as printers. Many older

CPU's could easily be connected as an output port for devices such as LCD and segment displays. This is due to the CPU having direct control of the terminals across the data bus. Here the CPU is able to control any number of peripherals as long as the format of the data is transferred according to the peripheral and the procedure used by the terminal. In this way it is possible to establish a number of devices across the same port. The diagram below identifies a standard connection across a multiple port connected to an analogue to digital input and a segment display. Here the system would read the values from the input and use this to output the decimal onto the segment display. The CPU would still need to run a programme to infer the response but it is possible to use the port in this way to run the application.

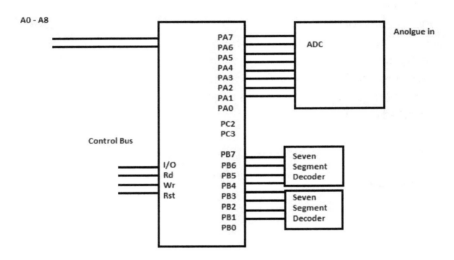

Fig 9.4.1 interface for a device across a terminal port

As can be seen the port simply uses the binary obtained from the data bus to run the installed devices. Although the connection is actually quite straight forward. The system itself might require a number of programming parameters. For instance the output to a segment display might require a data table which provides the binary responses to power the display unit. For instance an address table could be used to incorporate the correct outputs.

Address references for nested table

0 = 11111100	Address 0x64FF
1 = 01100000	Address 0x6501
2 = 11011010	Address 0x6402
3 = 11110010	Address 0x6403
4 = 01100110	Address 0x6404
5 = 10110110	Address 0x6405
6 = 10111110	Address 0x6406
7 = 11110000	Address 0x6407
8 = 11111110	Address 0x6408
9 = 11110110	Address 0x6409

It would be possible to use this table to output onto a peripheral connected to a port. The programme would simply need to refer to the table once a condition has been met. For example the ADC might be connected to a temperature display. The output would then need to correspond to the temperature provided by the ADC. The choice of the device connected determines what kind of program would need to run to create the expected output. This example demonstrates how versatile the connection to the port actually is and what can be achieved by wiring a device to the system

9.5.1 Designing an encoder for an I/O

The output from the I/O is typically completed in a binary format. For instance most 8 pin terminals are capable of providing a range of 0 – 255 expected outputs. Larger 64 bit systems can create even larger series of responses, which is dependent on the size of the data bus. This means that it is possible to connect the system to a peripheral which can interpret or send over 255 bytes of data. This concept can be explained using a typical keyboard. A keyboard uses something called ASII code which is an encoded sequence of binary which refers to the alphabet and a series of characters which are found on a keyboard. For instance the following code refers to the characters ABC.

A = 0000 0001
B = 0000 0010
C = 0000 0011

In fact the entire alphabet and a series of characters can all be written in ASCII binary. Meaning that each keypad press contains a binary equivalent output. The computer is able to use the binary and save the data into memory. An encoder is then able to perceive these letters as characters on a screen. But this is achieved by a different part of the computer. What the I/O does is merely send or receive the binary to an encoder such as a printer or Keyboard which is able to interpret the response. Encoders are necessary within computers as it is possible to encrypt or encode binary so that it can infer programmed patterns of response. The table for the segment display is just one form of encrypting binary. To obtain the entire 255 outputs the type of encoder needs to be quite specific to the binary state.

9.5.2 ASCII code in keyboards and printers

These devices are able to interpret information sent in binary and refer this to the equivalent alphabetical output. A printer needs to be able to understand the binary and print the expected character. A keyboard uses a different method which has series of wired connections which code a keypress into the correct binary output.

01000001	A	Capital A
01000010	B	Capital B
01000011	C	Capital C
01000100	D	Capital D
01000101	E	Capital E
01000110	F	Capital F
01000111	G	Capital G
01001000	H	Capital H
01001001	I	Capital I
01001010	J	Capital J

01001011	K	Capital K
01001100	L	Capital L
01001101	M	Capital M
01001110	N	Capital N
01001111	O	Capital O
01010000	P	Capital P
01010001	Q	Capital Q
01010010	R	Capital R
01010011	S	Capital S
01010100	T	Capital T
01010101	U	Capital U
01010110	V	Capital V
01010111	W	Capital W
01011000	X	Capital X
10110010	Y	Capital Y
01011010	Z	Capital Z

The system used to create the encoder for the peripheral consists of a series of digital logic gates which have bytes or inputs and a series of 255 expected responses or outputs. The information sent to the inputs would be decoded by the relevant digital pathways which create the responses expected on a truth table. To better explore this concept it is possible to use a keypad to explain the types of wiring found on the system.

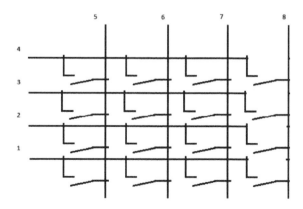

Fig 9.5.2 wiring found on a keypad

Here the keypad has ten push button switches which are able to create a separate Vcc signal output. If this is then fed to an encoder the signal sources can correspond with a 4 bit binary equivalent. This allows the output from the push button to be encoded as a binary signal. A connection made to the port of a computer would allow the binary to be interpreted by the CPU. This data could then be used within databases or memory space as well as to perform calculations or programming procedures. The table below shows the expected truth table for a 4 bit binary encoder.

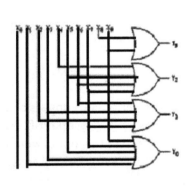

	Decimal	Binary
Q0	0	0000
Q1	1	0001
Q2	2	0010
Q3	3	0011
Q4	4	0100
Q5	5	0101
Q6	6	0110
Q7	7	0111
Q8	8	1000
Q9	9	1001

Fig 9.5.2 truth table and encoder for a 4 bit system

These types of processes are used a lot in peripheral access to the data bus. As an encoder would be used to create a number of signal sources into a binary format.

End of Chapter Quiz

What types of devices connect to an I/O?

Draw a wiring connection to a CPU port?

Describe the process used to initiate a data transfer?

Why do devices need an encoder to communicate in binary?

Designing I/O Procedures

In this chapter you will look at the following

- Identify types of devices and procedures
- Parallel and serial connections
- Creating simple procedures such as print and type
- Connecting other devices to an I/O

10.1.1 The basic functionality of an I/O system

In the previous chapter we looked at the types of devices which the interface can successfully connect with. Some devises are designed to work specifically for the computer, whilst other systems are able to connect as long as they able to run using the correct protocols. This process is actually quite simple as the interface is only able to commit to a limited range of functionality. Any device which is able to share the same bandwidth in bytes as the CPU is able to communicate to the system, in either a series or parallel data link. Which means that connecting to the system is quite possible using many types of peripherals. There are a number of reasons to connect a devise to the system, including data transfers, data manipulation as well as storage. Peripherals come in many types like today's gamer pads as well as scanners or automated systems. The CPU should be able to control any of these compatible devices.

REASONS FOR I/O INTERFACES

DATA TRANSFER	Sound/Visual
STORAGE	Scanner
DATA MANIPULATION	Automation
INTERACTIVE PROGRAMMING	

Table 10.1.1. Forms of I/O interface connections

Due to the compatibility of the I/O the device is actually able to connect to a number of systems, using the binary interface. Any connection still needs to create the data transfers in binary as most CPU's are only able to read information which is coded in this way. For this reason most type of devices or connections have a method of converting the binary information into meaningful data. For instance the encoder allows the CPU to control a keypad, it requires this form of encryption as the two devices do not normally use the same mode of communication. The device either needs an interface which the CPU is able to use, or contain an encoder which reads the binary sent from the system. The interface chosen to perform the data transfers is essential to the connection and uploading of data. Once the devices are able to communicate the CPU should be able to then perform a number of tasks which involve the manipulation and storage of data between the links.

10.1.2 Data protocols and device drivers

It is important to understand how the system works when it is transmitting data as the status and control register need to be programmed before it is able to create a link to the Ports. This is due to how information is transmitted between systems. For instance during a serial connection between a peripheral attached to a port and the CPU. The information would be sent over the port and decoded to 8 bit output before travelling across the data bus of the computers mother board. This process means that the peripheral during communication is using the same data bus as the CPU, and in this way is able to control the processes of the computer which it is attached to. During connections across the I/O interface it is possible to corrupt and damage data which is held on the system. Meaning that protocols are used to restrict information being transmitted across the bus and causing damage. The method used during the protocol is quite straight forward but depends on the devices being used.

Consider the following procedure. A device is connected to the PORTA of the I/O interface and the CPU needs to read the information which is being sent across the terminal. This procedure occurs in a number of stages. First the CPU provides a signal to the status register to confirm that it is ready to read the data. The device will then send the same byte to the status register which confirms the start of the data transfer. The following code identifies how this process is achieved.

Testing input

```
In A, INPUT
Bit 0, A
Jr Z, POLL
```

What is occurring is that a series of bytes called INPUT are being sent to the status register which turn the port into an input or receive state. The code INPUT will also notify the status register that the CPU is ready for the data transfer. The system will continue to repeat this process until a byte is recognised by the register and the process is able to begin. The repetition of the wait procedure is called POLLING and allows the system to continue to read the information on the status register until the devices are ready to connect.

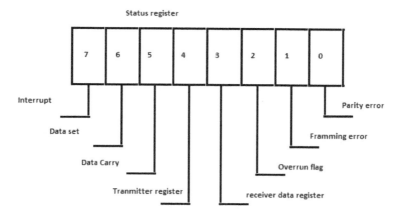

Fig 10.1.2 Diagram of a status register on an I/O port

The diagram above describes a basic set out of latches found on the status register of the I/O. These are used during interface protocols to determine processes such as interrupts and errors which might occur during a programme. These flags can be checked during code runtime as certain events need to establish how information is being sent. The control register works in a similar way but is responsible for deciding which operations are running at any point during a routine. The control is what determines the access to the data and address bus. Both registers are found inside the interface for the ports which provides the command signals while the interface is running.

10.2.1 Serial and parallel communication

The interface found on a computer, functions to send and receive information. Due to the types of transmission systems in common use there are a number of ways in which data moves between devices. For instance, binary data can be sent across terminals in what is called a serial transfer. This process sends information one byte at a time before moving onto the next word. This form of data transfer is useful if there are only a limited amount of space available to create transmissions lines on a data bus. This method is slower and less precise. But is still able to coordinate large data transfers. When information is sent in this way the data needs to store 8 bytes at a time and move the signals onto the data bus.

111

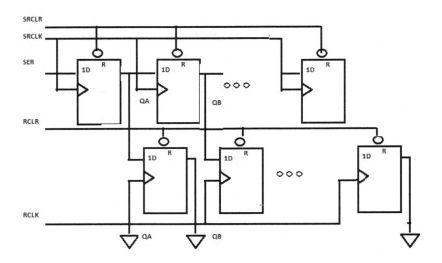

Fig 10.2.1 Serial in parallel out data bus

As can be seen in the diagram above the system reads each byte during the transmission, storing each byte onto a series of latches. When 8 bytes or one word has been achieved the system is able to transfer the word onto the data bus. A control signal is used to coordinate the movement of data between words. This method of sending binary is used in some systems with a limited data bus.

The second type of data transfer mentioned here is parallel communication. Which is similar form of interface except here the binary will be sent to the data bus byte for byte. Without the need for a complicated interface. Parallel terminals are merely the same bandwidth and are able to plug directly into the data bus of the secondary device. Parallel communication is preferred form for I/O interfaces and allows more information to be processed per second. Despite the similarities of the two methods the coding of a program depends on which form is chosen.

10.2.2 Programming parallel and serial connections

As mentioned, the coding of a programme depends on the type of communication transfer which is selected, as the CPU works differently depending on the mode. For instance when selecting serial communication, the register has to count each byte as it is received by the interface. This is easier to understand after looking at each type of coding. The below two sets of instructions highlight the differences in protocols which the CPU has to perform.

Parallel data communication example

```
Parallell
LD A, DATA            //Read count
Ld C, A               //Set count
SCHEDULE
In A, READY
Bit 5, A              //Check status of interface
Jr Z, SCHEDULE        //Jump to watch if not ready
PUSH AP               //Load stack
Dec C
Jr NZ                 //Finish when zero
```

In this line of code the program checks the status register, it then loads b with the memory space which it intends to use before beginning the transfer. Here the CPU only needs to inform the terminal that the program is ready for the download. This second line of code describes a similar process except the code is downloaded in serial bytes.

```
Serial
Ld C, 0               //Clear contents
Ld A, DATA            //Load b with byte count
LD B, A

Transfer
In A, INPUT
Bit 5, A
Jr Z, Transfer        //Read status
SRC A
LoopC A               //Ld A into c until 8 bytes
Jr Nc loop
```

These two examples highlight the different procedures which the CPU has to perform when completing a data transfer. Both methods load 8 bytes at a time into a memory location, except the serial communication needs to also count the bytes loaded into the register. So that it is able to check that 8 bytes are being processed at a time.

10.3.1 Common I/O procedures (print and type)

Some interface procedures are necessary to how the computer works, and for this reason have their own instruction set. This means that they either contain a call instruction which creates the procedure by running a protocol in memory. Or that extending formatting of the instruction allows a complex task to be carried out. For example the print instruction, is not actually a coded asm instruction. It is actually a number of programmes which allow the selected data to be sent to the I/O interface to connect with a computer. The reason for this is that some instructions do not need to be programmed into the computer but already exist as call procedures which runs the contents of the CPU's memory. This saves time during programming. But is also an example of programming used for common interfaces such as printers and keyboards. For instance certain compatible devices, will be hard wired into the programming of the computer to save developers' time.

It is also possible to design small programmes which are able to be called when using other types of interfaces. This merely pushes the memory location onto the stack and runs a routine found in the programme's memory location. The following code explores this process as the first routine 'print character' is used to print a string of letters in the second programme. Both sets of code are used within the printer module to print a series of letters.

The first programme tells the interface to print a character from memory location (String)

delay

```
In A (Test)
Bit 5, A                    //Test if ready
```

```
Jr Z delay
Ld A (String)            //Print memory location character
Out A
Return                   //Jump back to program
```

This programme is called in the next routine which prints a series of a string of characters. By calling the above routine a series of times. For example.

Print String

```
Ld B Decimal
Ld HP, Address1          //Load base address
Ld A, HP
Call STRING              //Print string
RNC HP
Dec B
Jr NZ Next
Return
```

Here the start value is the location in memory which indicates the start of the string. Number is the amount of letters found in the word which is due to be printed. The program prints each character and moves through the contents of the memory until each string is printed. Again it is possible to see that the wait instruction signals the interface to be ready by comparing the status register against a binary state. Before allowing the contents of the A register to move to the interface. This procedure is enough for the information to be sent to the printer.

This procedure can be considered a common interface as the binary information and code which signal the start of the new lines and words is identical to how the printer also understands the formatting of the computers page. The next programme is used for tele typing which uses the keyboard interface to store information on the computers screen. Again the programme uses a number of preformatted codes to create the screen print. This time the I/O interface is used as an input to receive the data.

Teletype

TeleTP

```
In A, STATUS
Bit 7, a
Jr Z ASC2              //Check status of interface
Call Delay 1
In A (ASC2)
Out ASC2, A
Call Delay 1
Ld B, 08H              //End of page
Nc A,(ASC2)
Out ASC2, A           //Print keyboard onto screen
SRC A,
RP c
Call Delay 1
Dec B
Jr Nl Poll
In A ASC2
Out ASC2, A
Call Delay 1
Return
```

How the procedure works is by polling the status register of the I/O interface. Which occurs after each delay. The information is read form the port and stored in the A register and loaded onto the screen. This occurs each time a key is presses. Also the cursor moves to the next screen bit each time a charter is printed to the screen.

10.4.1 Connecting other devices to an I/O

A computerised keyboard or printer can be easily interfaced to a CPU. The software will usually be written specifically for the application and will not need further assistance for it to work. The I/O interface actually offers a number of possibilities of potential applications of other devices, which need to be programmed for them to work. These devices which are found outside of the design of the system and can be integrated to the interface ports and operated from the CPU found inside the computer. Due to these types' of applications not being designed for the use of the system, the application may require extensive programming and forms of decoders for them to work. Programming other devices offers the 'user' a wider range of experiences form the CPU and other applications. This merely requires a peripheral and knowledge of the I/O protocols found on the computer.

POTENTIAL I/O APPLICATIONS	
AUTOMATED DEVICES	Relay systems
KEYPADS	PLC functions
LCD SCREENS	Control systems
SECURITY CONTROL	

Table 10.4.1 I/O applications

I/O interface can be quite easily designed, it is possible to start with simple applications which reads inputs and creates expected output responses. For instance a keypad could be used as a calculator or a segment display could be used to provide an output of water temperature for example. These types of devices are easily integrated to the port of a computer system by simply wiring the devices into the outputs of the ports. Due to the port having 8 possible outputs it is able to interact with a number of potential devices. Here designing a program for the system will depend on the number of inputs and what the program is expected to accomplish. For example an LCD screen will not need only the inputs for the devices control, it may also require the data connection to display the character outputs.

10.4.2 10.4.2 Interfacing a segment display

To demonstrate the application of the functionality of the CPU it is possible to describe how to wire a segment display to the system. The diagram below details the wiring of the device to the port. Here the

117

ports outputs are used to control the LED's in the segment display. The computer acts as the Vcc and the device is then connected to a ground. This should be enough to power the system and run a routine which uses the segment display to count down a number of numbers. The display itself can produce any number between 0-9 and letters A-F. By simply allowing a current to flow through the correct LED on the display. In this way a programme can be designed to create an expected sequence of outputs.

The following code is an example of how the port can be programmed to control the segment display. Depending on the binary sent to the port. Here the code is interchangeable in that the output to the display could have any number of potential outputs. For instance the outputs could either be in decimal or alphabetical characters.

```
LEDS
LD E, A              //A contains HEX digit
Ld D, 0
Ld HP, SegTab       //Use HL as index
Add HL, DE          //Tableaddress
LD A, (HP)          //Read code from table
LD B, 50h           //Delay value

Delay
OUT P, (A)          //Output set duration
Dec B               //Delay counter
Jr NZ, Delay        //Keep looping
Ld A, P             //C is port number
Dec P
CP LED1
Jr NZ, OUT
Ld BP, LED8
Ret
```

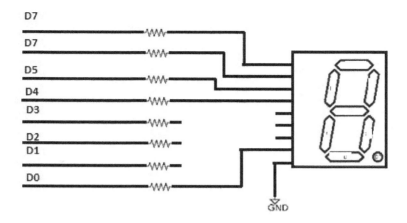

Fig 10.4.1 Wiring of a segment display to the port of a computer

The above code simply loads the contents of the memory address into port C from the A register. The memory address is then incremented and runs through each memory location until the entire sequence has been loaded into the output of the LED. The actual sequence which is stored inside the memory consists of a number of binary outputs intended for the seven-segment display. Once the sequence gets to the end of the base address the program disconnects for the output interface. This is one application of using the I/O port, but details how the CPU is able to control a secondary device from this peripheral. Due to the range of commands which the CPU is able to provide the interface can be used in a number of potential applications. Depending on the program used to run the system.

End of Chapter Quiz

List a number of I/O devices?

What is the difference between the serial and parallel port?

Design a protocol to connect a peripheral?

Create an application which uses its own program to command a device?

Sound on an 8 bit System

In this chapter you will look at the following

- Early forms of sound processing
- Programming an audio port
- Modern FPGA sound card
- Sound using multiple cores

11.1.1 Creating computerised audio

It is possible to create audio patterns using the CPU on a computer, although this is not completed by the CPU alone. Creating audio also includes a secondary chip which is able to be programmed to output the sound signals. During the runtime of a sound file the CPU is able to delegate commands which coordinate signals, but the actual sound processing needs to be completed through an encoder or device. This is then able to interpret the binary and output this into a relevant sound format. Due to the format in which files are saved to memory on a device. An audio file needs to be stored as binary data meaning that the file needs to be converted to binary and then decoded to the audio processor. This is relatively simple to complete as binary usually contains 8 bytes and the composition of a file will have 8 notes to convert. Once a file is saved in a relevant format the audio part of the signal is then able to be processed by the sound card or interface.

11.1.2 Sound processing using the Amstrad AY chip

Amstrad where one of the first devices to use a chip which was able to receive the binary data and output this into a simplified sound format. The audio it was able to produce was based around a beeper which could output a noise which could be modified in terms of its pitch and frequency. This formed the basis of the sound element of many of its pieces of software. Programming the device was very simple, as it had two registers for the output port. One is used to select the frequency, pitch and tone of an amplified signal to the speaker. The second is used to determine which port is being used as an output. For instance a single note can be created as a binary value and then reproduced by a speaker connected to one of the selected ports. This process takes two commands to achieve although each note has to be coded using the same format.

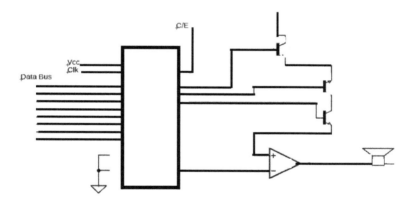

Fig 11.1.2 diagram of the connections to the Amstrad AY chip

As can be seen in the diagram above the interface for the chip and port is quite simple. The chip is wired to a data bus from the CPU and also an audio amplifier which is able to output the value once it has been interpreted by the system. For instance the 8 pins on the left of the chip are used as the data connection. The terminal on the other side of the chip is connected to a set of transistors which determine the frequency, tone and pitch of a single note. During a program the data will be decoded by the AY chip into the relevant output to the speaker. This is completed by modifying values received by the terminal to the chips register, and decoding the output through a MUX to the three output pins. The chip is interfaced directly to the data and control bus, which coordinates the movements of data as they are transmitted. The process of modifying the signal to a speaker completes the procedure of creating sound.

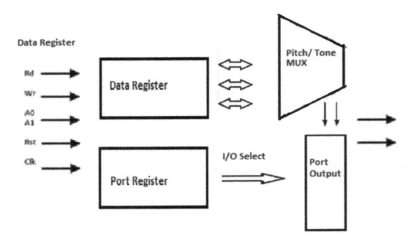

Fig 11.1.2 Block diagram of the AY chip

As well as the pinouts for the chip the IC also contains the registers for the pitch values and ports identification. The encoder connected to the data bus is used to modify the binary data. This creates the overall functionality of the sound card. Due to being one of the first sound chips, the model used by the Amstrad was simple and had very poor sound quality. It was simply unable to produce many sounds or create complicated music which included ranges of notes or effective uses of chords. This is due to the way in which it creates the audio output. It was simply limited in terms of achieving many notes and sounds at once. Instead the AY chip was used to modify and create its own sound wave patterns, which was unable to produce the expected outputs. One reason for his is the limited range of binary inputs, and also the production of sound was also ineffective when being used by the system. Modern computers have adapted the encoder for the data bus to include many more ranges of sound patterns and possible outputs. But this uses a different procedure to create this process.

11.2.1 Programming the AY sound chip

The block diagram of the AY chip identified the components found inside the device. The terminals and pinouts of the chip allow the circuit to connect to the data bus. This provides the transmission of signals between the speaker outputs and the binary stored in the memory. Most of these parts are irrelevant to running an application or programming the computer to produce sound. During a programme it is mainly the registers and ports which produce the changes in frequency of the sound. As mentioned the first register is used to modify the output to the speaker. The second register determines the port which is being used. The two registers are listed below.

Load port number: FFFD
Load data value: BFFD

The value to the right of the register is the address of the location where the register is found. This provides the data path for loading the value into the chip. This location works a lot like the memory in that the port is identified by the program counter which points to the correct address. Once the register is activated it is possible to determine how the note or frequency to the output is expected to behave. For instance loading a value into the data register will change the intended sound of the note. This is achieved by having three values across 8 bytes which set how the pitch, tone and the frequency of the beeper are distorted. The input to the register works in the following way.

PPTT FFDD   Where

P = Pitch
F = Frequency
T = Tone
D = Duration

Once the value is loaded to the data register the MUX is able to decipher the correct pitch of the note using a decoder which determines the tone and octave which is being outputted. The following code identifies how the expected sound wave is determined.

```
Push bc
Ld bc, &FFFD            //Select port register
Ld a, 0000 1111         //set port
Out C

Pop bc
Ld a, 10010011          //parameter for the note
Ld bc, &BFFD            //load register
Out c,a                 //output value
Return
```

The code represents a small programme to determine a single output to the audio amplifier located in the AY chip. The programme works by selecting the correct port by loading a value into register &FFFD. Then a second value is loaded into the register &BFFD which selects the pitch frequency and duration of the note. This process creates the expected sound output to the speaker, and is limited to producing a small number of outputs. During a programme the code provided above would need to be repeated for each note in the sound file. This would allow the CPU to interact with the port connected to the speaker. This process is now outdated as an audio file now has its own memory space for compiling sound files. The AY chip had to use this process as it was limited to using a sound wave distortion, rather than a sound card. Which meant that the CPU had to compile each stage in the audio signal. Given the range of an audio file, creating the template for a sound file would mean repeating the same process.

Despite the limitations of the port it is possible to programme effects into the sound file which broadens the range of outputs it is able to produce. For instance using repetition of notes and time distortions it is possible for the AY chip to change the way a sound file is played during runtime. Despite the lack of CPU commands with which the port is able to produce, it is still possible to use the effects and time distortions, to achieve a greater variety of response.

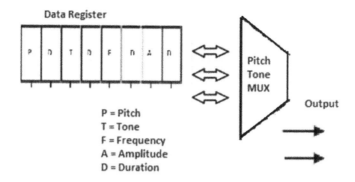

P = Pitch
T = Tone
F = Frequency
A = Amplitude
D = Duration

Fig 11.2.1 ADC used inside the MUX

11.3.1 Digital techniques of sound processing

Digital systems differ to analogue in the way that information is processed by the CPU. Due to the way the CPU coordinates information and processes data types. It is easier for the CPU to interpret binary and create sound forms by manipulating these types of patterns. It is possible to create sound out of binary data by using encoders and MUX's which make better use of sound and audio files. For instance the sound card which the Amstrad used was only able to output one note at a time. Making most common forms of sound outputs seem electronic. The design of the FGPA sound card allows the audio file to be reproduced in a better-quality format. For instance each note and chord can be written in binary and the FGPA responds by turning the binary data into the correct template for its audio equivalent. This allows the file to appear more natural to the original piece.

TYPES OF FPGA DESIGN	
PLC CONTROLLER	Spectrum analyser
GRAPHICS	Calculations
SOUND	Control interfaces
INPUT INTERFACES	

Table 11.3.1 FPGA application

11.3.2 Understanding an FPGA and its design

FPGAs are circuits which are able to take a set of inputs and repeat a process which manipulates the data. These types of devices are used when calculations or transformations of data need to occur at a fast rate. For instance graphics cards are able to take 16 bytes of graphical information on an image and improve the binary to 256. This process can be achieved in a number of ways, depending on the design of the FPGA. For instance some graphics cards are used to convert the bit rate. While others are able to complete image and texture alterations to image files. As the CPU is expected to repeat a number of similar processes. It is possible to achieve this using an FPGA board design, which contains the hard written digital logic. The digital logic is designed in such a way in which it can be programmed to complete different tasks at a faster rate than the CPU.

The FPGA circuit is designed to manipulate and output the data, rather than waiting for programmed command signals. This means that data files can be compressed to only contain relevant data rather than huge amounts of specific code. The design of the sound card outputs the data file in better quality and can also reproduce greater ranges of notes and chords, at the same time, as it makes better use of data and address buses. The design of the FPGA is actually quite simple and depends on the uses and functionalities of the board. It is possible to demonstrate this by planning a simplified version of an FPGA card

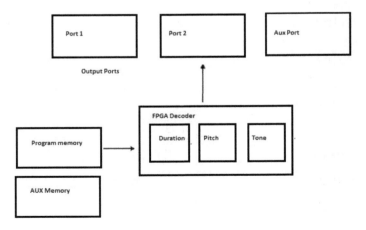

Fig 11.3.2 Block diagram of FPGA sound card

The block diagram above identifies the process and components needed in the FPGA board. For instance there are a number of registers which determine, which process the card is currently completing. For instance the port can be set to read data and either produce a range of electronic outputs, or manipulate the data into better quality format. This is achieved by setting the value in the status register. The card can also use an 8 byte data connection to provide 256 responses. Which means that the controller can not only produce a pattern of notes, it is also possible for the sound file to create a sequence of chords at the same time. This is achieved by the MUX and encoder which is connected to the data bus, which determines how the data is then processed. Due to the possibilities of design it is actually possible that the FPGA board is able to achieve more responses. Depending on the intentions of the board.

As the FPGA uses an encoder it is necessary to identify how the data is expected to be decoded. The code below explores how the binary can be used to create a type of sound format.

1110 00111
CCDD NNDD

C = Chord
N = Note
D = Duration

In the example above the chords and notes are written in two bytes, meaning there are 8 possible outputs. The second part of the code determines the duration of the current note. This is one possible design. Although different formats identify different ways of coding which need to identify issues such as tempo and ranges of sound. The FPGA can be designed to interpret huge ranges of data and improve the quality of the sound file.

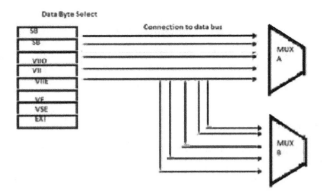

Fig 11.3.2 An encoder connected to the data bus of a sound card

The image above describes how the data bus is connected to the encoder found in the FPGA. What occurs is that the data is sent directly from the audio file found on the memory straight to the input of the data bus, rather than being sent through the CPU. Here the MUX is used instead of the CPU to complete the calculations used to derive the audio format. Once the information is on the data bus, the MUX selects the correct process according to the current instruction found on the status register. The encoder can then provide correct method of data manipulation and produce the intended output. Here the MUX is used to decide which note and chord is being played according to the instruction received in binary. The MUX is designed to then send the expected output to the speaker. This design only uses 8 bytes and is actually quite simple, although it would be possible to improve the system by broadening the range of programmed responses.

11.4.1 Developments in sound processing

The FPGA allowed sound processing to include multiple channels from direct digital to sound conversion. Using this method allows a binary sequence to be processed by the circuit and coded directly into its equivalent sound wave. For instance the Amstrad was able to achieve a signal note by changing the pitch and tone of the beepers sound wave. The FPGA uses an encoder to achieve this through multiple channels. Here the binary programme corresponds directly to a corresponding wave form. Which produces a greater range of sounds. The diagram below identifies a circuit used to create an alteration in a sound wave. This can then be further manipulated until the structure of a sound image is created. The circuit below merely alters the pitch on a sound signal caught on an electrical current. On an FPGA board there are many of these circuits which are able to produce the many types and variations in effects.

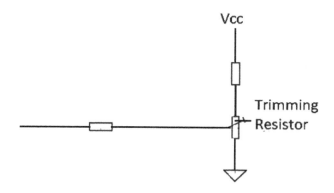

Fig: 11.4.1 circuit to alter the pitch of a sound wave

11.4.2 Sound processing in multiple cores

The FPGA means that more information is conveyed in an audio file, as it is possible to create a program without using chunks of programmed code. This also meant that due to the demand on the CPU when the programme is running. Audio files now have their own memory destination during runtime. This is because of timing issues of events being coordinated which also needs access to the data bus and the output interface etc. It is actually difficult to get the programme to process different events at the same time. Which meant that the audio interface has been designed so that it is separated from the other parts of the system. For this reason when the computer processes an audio file the data is loaded from the memory location to a space in the RAM which is used to process audio information. Using this method. The file is saved and has direct access to the audio port. This means that other programmes are able to interact with the CPU without stalling the software.

Dual core processes allow the CPU to be accessed by a number of systems such as the audio drive during runtime. This process also means that sound files are programmed in a different way to the AY chip. Here the CPU is used to select the memory location, and run the sound file. Once the path is adapted in the programme. The CPU can then be used by other processes and returns back to the previous location in the stack register. For instance.

```
RequestSound
Ld, A StatB
Bit 7
Call RequestSound
Jr Nz
```

```
Datafile
Mov a, 42FF          //memory address of sound image
Out                  //Output
Inc A
Jr, 45FF             //Location of the end of the file
return
```

Here the file is sent to the RAM location used by the audio interface and outputs the values found in the binary via the FPGA. The audio interface will be able to read the binary and reproduce the audio format found in the file. The programme will load the entire contents into the RAM before it is output to the audio interface. This method allows for better use of the CPU, as it does not need code to output each point in the sound file.

End of Chapter Quiz

Describe a circuit to output a sound wave?

How do FPGA and DSP systems differ?

What are the differences in programming between the two systems?

Design an encoder used by an FPGA design?

Display and Image Processing

In this chapter you will look at the following

- Defining display and image processing
- How a computer system processes images
- Identify components used by the system
- Programming an image

12.1.1 What is image processing?

Modern digital techniques are able to use a number of ways to digitally capture an image. For instance cameras and computer displays are able to create a digital likeness of an image. This works by identifying each pixel on a screen and providing a binary coordinate which is able to describe the entire picture. There are a number of formats which these images are produced in, including standard png files and PDFs. The quality of the images may depend on the type of process which is used to store the image. Once the image is converted to binary it is possible to alter the quality and style of the image by changing the ways the pixels are aligned. Such as colour and texturizing edits, as well as adding more details to the document. The storage and conversion of picture images to binary formats means that many types of images can be edited and redesigned for use in other types of formats and software.

Image processing refers to binary files which are coded picture documents. Display and video processing is slightly different as the binary has to capture a moving image. For this reason the document has to be stored in other forms such as tape and magnetic disk. This is due to the size of the file and the difficulty of storing the images as single bytes.

These differences in picture formats mean that they are processed in different ways by a computer system. Some forms rely on external drives which are able to handle the size of the documents. Whereas the system inside the computer is still able to process smaller image files, which are stored in binary. The process used by the computer depends on the format in which the picture is presented. The following descriptions refer mainly to image processing as this method best illustrates processes such as screen representation and software techniques.

12.1.2 Storing a digital image

Using a computer system, the image is comprised of a number of binary references referring to the pixels found on a screen. Early formats used a full pixel black and white image. Or lower resolution colour format which displayed half as many pixels. This was due to saving space on the computer's hard drive. The image itself is created using a series of x y coordinates which list the entire size of the screens display. The quality of the picture obviously depends on the resolution of the image and how the file is formatted. The table below describes how a simple image might appear as a series of binary. As the image is read one series of binary at a time. The processor moves from left to right until the entire image is processed to the TFT display, each pixel at a time. The timing rate of the frame depends on the processors clock and the oscillator found in the displays control unit. The image itself will just be comprised of a number of binary states as found in the table.

X/Y	1	2	3	4
1	255	36	124	213
2	45	25	75	123
3	34	44	168	188
4	233	211	200	23

Table 12.1.2 an image displayed as a number of binary references

Here the picture quality would be expected to be above average as an entire 255 bytes are used per pixel meaning that the resolution would be able to handle colour processing. It is also necessary to point out that the data byte is presented as a series or X and Y coordinates, which allow the system to scan across the data file and output a picture onto the display unit or TFT. The output is created moving the image across the visual processors data buffer which feeds the bytes to a decoder which is able to produce a colour or black and white image depending on the screen. The diagram below considers the movement of data across the data bus into the various colour outputs located on the screen. The transfer of information depends on the frame rate and the time it takes for each line of display resolution to send onto the screen. This works by scanning across the X, Y coordinates until the image appears on the display.

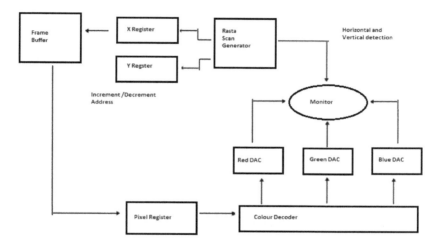

Fig 12.1.2 transfer of data across the data buffer

12.2.1 How a computer system processes images

The visual system for a computer is quite similar to the processing of sound, in that the system allots some memory to the display and visual processes. This might be a separate or joined system which has at least enough space to provide an output for the display module. The earlier systems used a display resolution of 256 x 192 meaning that the memory for the display had to be at least 6800 bytes. This allowed for the screen to display a picture quality image. Here the memory would have its own address location on the bus and any information found in the memory address would appear on the screen. Depending on the system the visual unit may also contain processors which are able to modify images and create effects for the keyboard and mouse etc. Many modern systems integrate other peripherals and are able to delegate and process numbers of tasks to output on a display.

Creating memory locations on the address bus

&0001 – 2FFF Program space
&3000 – 5FFF Memory
&6000 – 7FFF Sound
&8000 – 9FFF Display

The visual system is connected to the bus like most other devices in that it shares the bus with the control unit and CPU. Meaning that either component is able to interact with the visual and display unit. In this way the CPU is able to create control of the device during programmed routines and also interact with the memory. The display system also has its own processor, but due to the way commands are coordinated across the bus. The visual unit needs these controls to perform the required instruction set about by the programme. For instance the keyboard might need to write onto the display. Or the cursor needs to gain access or point to another part of the program. The diagram below describes the interaction of the CPU and memory to the visual display unit.

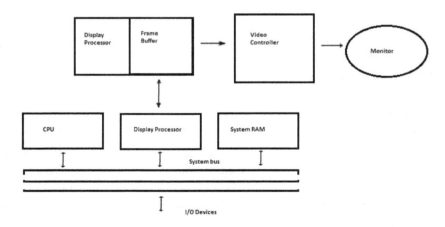

Fig 12.2.1 block diagram of data across the bus

12.2.2 The processor inside the display unit

As mentioned, the display unit not only contains the memory address for the display output. There is also a processor inside the system which is able to delegate and control the procedures which the visual system has to decode. This component works in a number of ways, for instance the processor has to interact with peripherals connected to the device as well as generating images onto the screen. These processes need to be controlled by one device which is responsible for the timing and output to the display. The display module controls three main types of procedures such as the controller, generator and console. The first part interacts with the CPU to provide the interrupt signals to the display and handles the instructions sent across the data bus. The controller coordinates the events which have access to the display, and processes any instructions which mean that the display needs to interact with the programme. For instance the CPU might tell the system to input a few characters onto the screen. The controller will be the first part of the system which decodes this command, by selecting the relevant system and address.

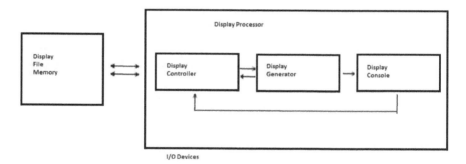

Fig 12.2.2 components found in the display processor

The second part of the sysem interacts with the programmes and peripherals attached to the computer. For instance the display generator is a tye of encoder which creates process which are specific to the computer terminal it is based on. The display generator interacts with the keybard and ASCII code to write the characters into the display. There may also be another part of the system which creates procedures which are used to draw images onto the systems memory. Some software might use this part to create the image of a circle onto a document. The image generator works alot like a decoder which is able to infer the output to an instruction, by selecting the correct process to use when outputting the outcome of the procedure. Again this part needs to access information across the data bus and uses the processor found in the controller to complete the procedure. This device allows the peripherals found on a computer to interact with the output sent to the images display.

The final part of the processor is the display console. This part of the device allows a peripheral to select a location of the display to write onto the memory. Again this part is used in conjunction with the keyboard and mouse to select and write into the memory address. It is also possible to use the console to interact with the ROM so that the computer is able to run and control commands from prompts found on the screen. The console works by decoding the coordinate on the screen to the correct part in the systems memory. Which allows the 'user' to interact with devices which are able to provide inputs onto the display and memory.

12.2.3 Adding a peripheral to the display unit

Due to the visual system having its own processor it is possible to add devices to the system which are able to directly interact with the display. Here the processor is used to coordinate the signals which allow a secondary device to control the screen or part of it. For instance a TV signal or camera is able to gain access to the data buffer which controls the screen temporariliy during certain command processses. Here a signal would provide a que to the interrput in the control unit, before allowing the secondary device access to the data buffer. The processor would control the procdures which are sent directly from the ROM to the data bus. The camera would then be used by the port and have the chance to interact with certain programmes. Using this procedure it would be possible to edit an image once it has been translated into binary in the systems memory. In fact there are a number of software procedures which are able to change the texture and quality of stored image files.

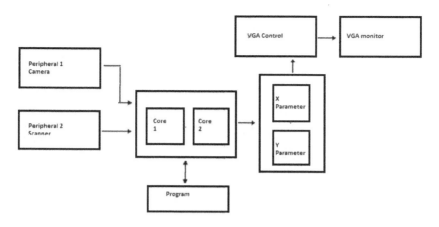

Fig 12.2.3 using a processor to add a camera function

12.3.1 Controlling the screen output using programmed commands

Like most systems in a computer it is necessary to use commands to create or programme an output for the system. The format of the command range is actually quite simple, as the computer is only set to provide a limited range of programmable responses. As mentioned, the cursor is one of the simplest commands in use, which is again controlled by the display console inside the visual processor. Here it is possible to move from one part of the screen position and enter the code in the screen. This is used when the keyboard is selected to move the character letters onto the screen image. The polling for this event in the screen editor occurs in the following format.

ReqChar

```
Push BC
Push HP
Ld A, 0
Call &16FF          //Opens channel 2 for the keyboard input
Pop AF
Call &15D4          //Reads character form keyboard
Pop BP
Pop HP
```

```
PrintASC2
Ld A,2
Call &1601
RPT 2                   //Prints character


Move Cursor
Ld A, 22                //character position for cursor
RCP 2


MoveText
Ld A, 13                //Moves the position of the cursor
Return
```

Another function which the processor is able to perform is loading an image onto the screen. This is achieved line by line on an X, Y coordinate. A series of call functions allow the bytes to be input onto the correct screen position. The following code represents how the screen loads each screen position.

```
ScreenCol 24 equ 1000
ScreenWidth 522 equ 255  //set screen parameters


Call ClearScreen        //Clear screen and load position
Ld BC, &C0000
Call MovScreenWidth     //Move across screen width
Ld b, 255
Again:
SetByte b
Dec b
Ld A,B
And %00001111
Jr Nz,
Call MoveText          //The data is found here
```

Calling this program infers the image onto the screen using the visual processor to direct the information onto the VRAM. The last program here is used to call a sprites movement across the VRAM. It is also possible to use this same function to move a tile or image on the screen. I.e. during some forms of gameplay a tiled image needs to move on the screen between points. Which allows the screen image to become interactive.

```
NewSpriteChar
Ld HL, &C80FF: LinePos 2.
Ld A,H
Add &CFF
Ld H,A
Bit 5, h
Jp Nz
Push BC
MoveNextLine:
Ld ScreenPos HP,
Return
```

Here function calls the image of the screen sprite and creates a macro which moves the sprites character to the VRAM calling each line of the sprite. This allows the image to move across the VRAM memory space. These programs identify how the screen processes images and allows an output to be placed onto the screens VRAM. As mentioned, the processor in the visual unit is used to complete this process. The access from the data bus allows the CPU to call command functions to the unit. But the system is designed to have its own core so that it is able to respond in a similar way to the audio unit, in that it needs to react separately to this part of the system for it to work. Again the functionality of the visual unit depends on what tasks it is being asked to perform, as some units have their own set of programmed responses and peripherals.

End of Chapter Quiz

Describe the processes used in a visual unit?

How would a processor be programmed to identify an area of the screen?

What processes are separate from the central CPU?

What types of peripherals have access to the screen?

Part 3

CPU Structures and Design

13

Designing a Simple CPU

In this chapter you will look at the following

- Structures inside a CPU
- Designing the functionality
- Identifying address requests
- Understanding procedures

13.1.1 Structures found in a CPU

Designing a CPU is dependant on the processes which the computer is expected to perform. The CPU itself is the part of the computer which manipulates the data and controls the other parts of the system. The computer depends on the logic states the processor can achieve to complete these tasks. For this reason computers do not necessarily share the same format or structure in terms of their design. For instance a small calculator will not be expected to perform tasks which involve editing visual information. This would mean that the calculator is unable to process the same types of data and the instructions addressing would not be able to be used on the secondary device. Another difference between these machines is that the calculator would also not have the interfaces or data paths which would be used to process the VGA signals. This would be because the processors are not designed in the same way.

For this reason designing a CPU means identifying the applications and purposes needed to complete the commands. It also means designing the structures which are able to infer the binary into the meaningful data. A calculator for example would need to include an ALU which is able to complete the expected mathematical procedures. The data would also need to be stored and moved between locations. For this reason the device would also need a series of registers and accumulators which the binary is able to be manipulated in. The structures found in a CPU are dependent on the intentions of the device. There is not a rule on the method used to create a CPU and many types uses different procedures which are variations on other models. The CPU can be designed in a number of ways as long as it is able to complete the expected tasks for the device. Despite methods for the computers design being different there are similarities between the structures which exist inside the CPU.

BASIC CPU STRUCTURES

ALU	Addressing
CONTROL UNIT	Shift register
REGISTERS	Counters
BUSES	I/O

Table 13.1.1 basic CPU principles

At a very simple level a CPU would merely contain a number of registers, for moving data. There would also be an addressing procedure and control unit to decode the binary instructions. The input to the device is completed either from memory or though the interface to the I/O port. This would provide the programmed code needed to move the data. The final part of the CPU would be the ALU or structures needed to perform the calculations. On computers such FPGA boards. This is a series of digital logic gates which coordinate binary information into graphical visual outputs. The design of the unit depends on how these processes are coordinated and the contexts in which they are used. For instance the memory on the chip is usually located in a separate IC. This makes it easier to separate some of the processes, spending more time on creating larger instruction sets. The unit might also need a control board as some processes are expected to be performed at the same time of others. It simple depends on the system

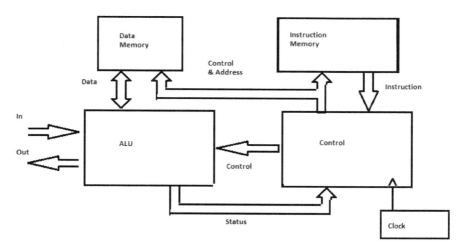

Fig 13.1.1 Structure of a CPU

The diagram above describes the basic assumptions which are used to create a simple CPU control system. Most of the processes have been described in the book. It is possible to use this schema to design a computer with a limited set of responses.

13.2.1 Designing a simple system

To design a system it is necessary to identify the purposes and intentions of the computer. For example if the computer is used to process the responses of various inputs to react if differences are found to the expected output. Then, the instruction set would need to include instructions which can compare signals and provide the correct adjustment or reaction from the processor. The CPU has to be designed to respond in this way. Other questions exist in the design phase such as instruction sets and potential programming queries. The CPU should be able to function at the level it is intended to work at.

13.2.2 8 bit input CPU design

To better understand the construction of a CPU it is possible to design a small application which allows the concepts to be tested in terms of a working model. The CPU is designed around the following premise.

"The device has a 4 bit calculator which can either process information from memory or an input to the device. The CPU can also output the information to a module or interface such as a display."

The processes here are very uncomplicated. The CPU merely takes two binary values and outputs the value to a device. The algorithm can also jump between parts of the program, depending on what the programme is trying to do. The expectation is that the CPU can be programmed to create a number of patterns depending on the information that is input to the device. Here the CPU can be reprogrammed to complete a number of different tasks. The idea is to achieve the design without too many complicated processes needed to create the device. The program itself would be loaded onto the systems memory and the CPU is then able to decode the relevant commands.

The diagram below is a block diagram of the components found within the CPU. For instance the CPU has an arithmetic unit which uses two registers and an accumulator to perform the calculations on the binary. The processor also has an interface for the I/O control and a number of digital logic gates which are used to jump between sequences on the program counter. The Diagram also details the movement of data across the CPU.

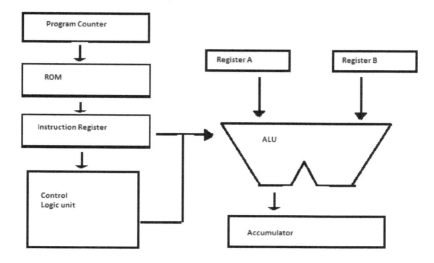

Fig 13.2.1 Design of the 8 bit CPU

As can be seen the module consists of a number of registers and a control unit system which reads and decodes the instructions addresses. The CPU also has access to the memory and I/O interface which allows the system to interpret data from either device. Depending on the programme which is being run at the time the data will be loaded to the CPU from either device. The design of the system is actually quite straight forward as many of the systems are possible to recreate using a series of logic gates or transistor pathways.

13.3.1 Creating the instruction address procedures

The CPU is designed around 16 instructions from a 4 bit decoder. This allows the CPU to use four inputs to decode a maximum of 16 instructions. The data is still in 8 bit meaning the maximum value of the machine is limited to an output of 255 decimal. Any value larger than this would update a carry flag on the status register. This means that the address bus is 12 bytes in length which include the information for the instruction as well as the data line. Instructions which do not carry any numerical value could will be left as blank. Although it is possible to change this system to a MUX which could reduce the instruction list to 8 bytes. Depending on the design of the system. The instruction found on the CPU are listed below.

List of the CPU instructions.

Calculations:
Add subtract
Compare
Increment

Jump statements:
Push stack
Pop stack
Call address
Jump if zero

Load:
Exchange contents of registers
Load register A
Load register B
Load and increment

Input output interface:
Load A from Input
Load B from input
Output register A
Output register B

These instructions from the addresses found in the 4 bit register decoder. The instructions are grouped in to four types of processes which simplifies the wiring of the control unit. Here the four groups each have their own process inside the control unit as each group uses the same data paths. Here the control unit has a 5 part counter timer, meaning that each instruction takes 5 clock signals to complete. This allows the control unit to select the correct data path as it moves across the system. Grouping the statements together also allows the instructions to be coded for conditional jump sequences as the status register is able to compare the value of the group alongside the current value to determine when conditions are being met. The below groups of binary indicate the references used to group the instructions.

0000-0011	Arithmetic
0111- 0111	Jump instructions
1000- 1011	Load instructions
1100– 1111	I/O instructions

As mentioned these values are used by the control unit to decipher each instruction. The control works by creating a logic sequence which infers the correct data path for the instruction. A typical sequence would follow the following procedure which is used to code the instruction.

Clock time	Procedure
To	Point program counter at memory
T1	Load instruction to instruction register
T2	Fetch instruction
T3	Decode instruction
T4	Increment program counter

Table 13.3.1 standard timing cycle for basic CPU

As can be seen the clock timer signals the control unit to move the data across the control bus, which selects the correct system. During the fetch and decode cycle the sequence interacts with the type of command which is currently being decoded. The address which is selected by the unit depends on the grouping of the instruction. Here the correct data path depends on how the CPU responds to the instruction. The diagram below describes the interaction of the system according to each instruction.

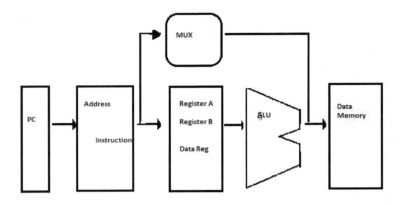

Fig 13.3.1 Identifying instruction addresses

13.3.2 Creating the wiring interface for the system

To better understand how the PCB of the design can be implemented, it is possible to describe a wiring diagram for this system, which details how the CPU and port interface are wired in terms of the input ports to each chip. The diagram below describes the entire systems wiring. So that the CPU and memory are able to interact with the access to the external ports. The system itself relies on the address and control bus to move the data around the system. The CPU is obviously split into the separate control units and ALU calculation device. The wiring diagram stated here only provides access to the wiring chart and not the specific detail to the logic found in the integrated units.

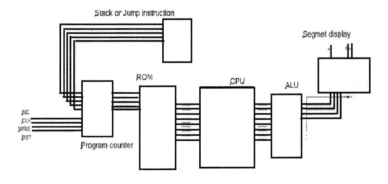

Fig 13.3.2 Wiring diagram of the CPU

13.3.3 Creating a jump procedure

As well as creating calculations the CPU is expected to be able to jump between protocols in the programme according to information received form the status register. The status register sets a flag each time a value a compare function is considered true. For example a flag is set each time two values are equal to the other. For instance if two binary values stored in the registers are the same value then a flag is set in the status register. This is designed as a series of D flip flops where state has its own flag. The conditional jump sequence is able to occur when both the flag is set and the instruction requests the command. To achieve this a series of logic gates are attached to the status register and the control units' decoder. The diagram below identifies this process.

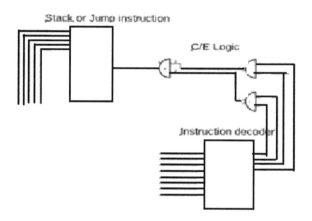

Fig 13.3.3 Jump sequence digital logic

When the jump procedure occurs the address of the routine is popped from the stack into the program counter which creates the jump to the next routine. This is due to how the stack is able to change the pointer in the program counter and move the instruction to the next address. The program counter returns to the previous point in the programme, as the return address is memorised by the stack.

13.4.1 Using the CPU to create procedures

The design and structure of the CPU should be enough to understand how the processes are expected to work under simulation. The processes of the control unit and addressing registers have been identified, meaning that it is possible to now develop code which is able to use the binary which forms the instructions. As stated the instructions are written in 12 bytes which include 4 bits for the instruction and a further 8 bit data use to carry the numerical values. The data bus to the address register and the CPU are both 12 bytes long for this reason. Given this terminology for the instruction set it is now possible to identify a few procedures aimed at using the structure of the CPU. Below are two programmes created to manipulate the data using the CPU.

Exercise 1:

This programme reads the input port and stores the result in the register. The calculation during the programme is used to display an output.

Programme 1:

```
Rd a,              //reads port
Ld a,
Rd a,
Ld b,
Sub a,b            //perfroms calculation
Ld accumulator
Output a,
```

Exercise 2:

This programme again loads two inputs but this time the type of calculation is selected by the input received from the port.

Programme 2:

```
Rd a               //Loads value form Ports
Ld a
```

Rd b,
Compare 001   //Checks status register
BTSFC
Jump Sub
Jump Add

Add   //Add operation
Rd a
Ld b
Add a,b
Output Acc

Sub   //Subtract operation
Rd a,
Ld b,
Sub
Output Acc

End of Chapter Quiz

Design a CPU system?

What interfaces are used by the CPU?

Design a system with memory and without?

How is it possible to create a programme without a read only memory?

14

Designing an FPGA System

In this chapter you will look at the following

- Applications of FPGAs
- Describe a range of procedures
- Designing an FPGA
- Interfacing the components

14.1.1 FPGA applications

FPGAs are systems which are able to coordinate processes which tend to repeat themselves. This differs from a CPU as a computer processor is programmable and needs to be dynamic to a range of commands. FPGAs are used to conduct the same procedure again and again. For instance a spectrum analyser for a radio or sound device needs to be able to continually select the same signals from a multitude of potential inputs. The FPGA is used to repeat the same process. Selecting the correct signal each time it is requested. These types of devices are used a lot in computerised systems as they are able to be used in a number of systems to create quick calculations a processor is then able to respond to. In fact FPGAs are a common interface to use in a range of devices and it is possible to design a system for many types of use.

Within computerised systems FPGAs are used for the resolution of the monitor display as well as coordinating signals to the sound card. Here the FPGA would take a graphical input and alter the resolution depending on the type of output which is requested. For instance a graphics card contains a number of encoders and digital systems which are able to change binary into colours which are used on the pallet for the display.

The encoders take the binary inputs and create a calculation which amends the displays output. Designing an FPGA is similar to creating a processor except the system usually needs an interface with a number of I/O ports. To better explain how this system is used in a computer it possible to identify the processes which occur in an audio example.

14.1.2 Creating an FPGA application

The intention of the FPGA is to convert binary into a sound output on the systems audio card. The FPGA needs to be able to convert the information from a binary file into a number of channels, which allow the output to contain a greater depth of sound. This differs from a standard audio wave in that the output usually has only one expected channel. Meaning that an audio output is able to be created using the systems software. The application for the FPGA can be achieved by using a processor and a number of encoded channels which decode the information sent from the memory. The block diagram below identifies the structure of the sound card. Here the system reads the information from the ROM or VRAM and uses a processor to output the file through the multiple channel encoders. The channels take the binary and uses the tone generators to create the sound wave. There is also an ADC which is able to convert an incoming signal into a digital format.

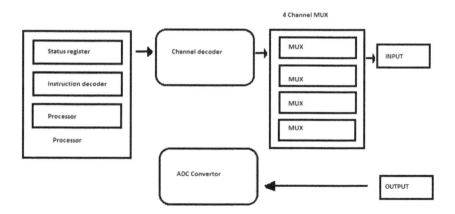

Fig 14.1.2 diagram of the FPGAs structure

The diagram identifies the structure of the system. The processor is used to decode the program and move the data into the relevant channels. There is also a status register in the processor core which is used for polling and coordinating the procedures and interrupts. The sound card is interfaced directly into the systems I/O ports for connections to the speakers and audio input. The bulk of the audio processing is found in the channels which interpret the binary using a tone generator.

14.2.1 Addressing and the instruction format

The sound card is interfaced directly to the data bus meaning that like the CPU it is able to contain a number of instructions. The intention is that the address register is then able to select a number of processes to move the data to the intended output. The data file itself is expected to load into the extended RAM and move into the outputted channels. This occurs by polling the system and responding when the data bus is not in use. Once loaded the data can then be transferred to the relevant outputted channels. The commands only need 4 bytes to ceat the expected number of instructions. These are detailed below.

0001 - Wait command which determines if the program is in use
0010 - Transfer instruction to VRAM
0011 - 2 output types standard and digital
0100 - Register determines whether device is input or output

There is also a D flip flop register which determines the status of the device. During the runtime of a program creating a compare function against the status register determines the current instruction. This is useful during polling or identifying if a process is being carried out.

Byte 1- Ready to transfer
Byte 2 – Output in use
Byte 3 – Input in use
Byte 4 – Digital output
Byte 5 – Standard output
Byte 6 – ADC transfer

The final part of the instruction is how it is decoded by the device. Here the system does not actually use the standard format of data and instruction. This is due to the way the device handles information. The data is first downloaded to the VRAM and the entire code is held in data format. Due to the application of the encoders the data has its organisation and is able to be streamed directly to the output from the FPGA. The data is organised in the following structure.

Opcode Channel	Operand
Select Chanel	Data type

Here the data passes through the processor and selects the relevant MUX channel. This then encodes the data type through the tone generator producing the correct response in the audio output channel. This gives the sound wave its quality and infers the duration and structure of the note. For instance one channel contains chord structure; and another notes. There is also an MUX for effects and distortions.

14.3.1 Identifying the structures n the FPGA

The FPGA is essentially a programmable calculation device. In that it is able to use commands to change the expected output from the data terminal. Again the FPGA works by using encoders to quickly decrypt a file and decode the inputted data. This is achieved in the sound card through the use of a processor and a number of other structures. The diagram below identifies the addressing decoder used by the CPU to infer the instruction from the data bus and process the intended command. This part of the sound card is similar to the CPU in that it has a control and addressed data input. The component is able to identify the instruction and move the data to the relevant part of the FPGA.

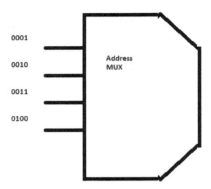

Fig 14.3.1 diagram of addressing MUX

The status register works alongside the addressing processor to interpret the current use of the FPGA and determine which processes are then able to be carried out. This is achieved by a series of digital logic structure which stop other processes occurring during run time. I.e if there is a positive signal in the transfer byte of the status register, this will mean that other responses are unable to be processed during this request. For any event to occur in the sound card the program has to compare the polling byte so that the CPU can determine if the register is ready to move on to the specified task.

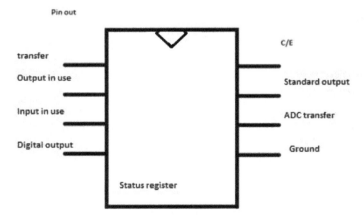

Fig 14.3.1 diagram of a status register

Once the status register has determined that the I/O interface is ready to transfer digitally. The VRAM sends the data stored in the memory to the encoders which are able to process the digital information into a sound wave. This occurs through each channel having three inputs which determines the note or chord, and a further two inputs which detemine pitch and duration. Across the four channels it is able to produce a range of output and effects which the FPGA outputs from the saved data file.

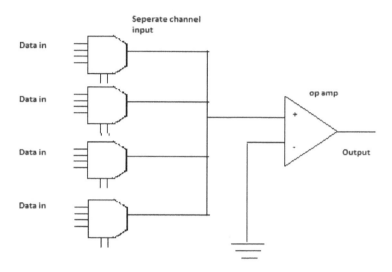

Fig 14.3.1 diagram of encoder channels

The final components found on the device are the I/O interface, VRAM and ADC. The port interface selects the state of the port, i.e. input or output as well as the resolution of the signal being transmitted. This is again an integrated chip which has a single input which can be divided into a number of ports. It is also possible to control the interface from the CPU so that the relevant command is then selected. The port interface separates the audio system from other parts of the computer and any specified peripherals. The VRAM is basically a designated chunk of memory which has its own address locations so that it is possible for the program to identify the location of a memory file. The final component is an ADC which is a type of analogue to digital convertor that processes incoming audio and manipulates the signal by converting it to a digital format. This is then transmitted to the VRAM where it can then be loaded into memory.

14.3.2 The control unit completing a procedure

The control unit in the processor of the FPGA works in a similar step of procedures to the CPU in the computer system. The instruction is still decoded before the relevant component is selected by the control unit. The program counter also needs to be able to point at the relevant address. The exception is that once the transmission of data has been initiated the data file is run through the decoder a lot like a string of characters, so that the entire file is passed through the system. The sound card is then unable to process further information during this procedure unless an interrupt has been initiated by another program. This is signified by the status register receiving a set of signals from the instruction decoder. The process of the control unit is stated below

Clock time	Procedure
To	Load instruction to instruction register
T1	check status register
T2	Fetch instruction/
T3	Decode instruction
T4	Wait for interrupt or poll

Table 14.3.2 timing procedure for basic FPGA board

The process is still completed by the control unit in the CPU, except the FPGA takes over once the file is downloaded. The file is then downloaded and the next instruction would load the file through the sound processing unit. The FPGA has its own processor as the output needs to occur at the same time as other running programs. This means that other components such as the memory only need to share the data bus when the two devices are interacting.

14.4.1 Procedures for programming the device

The decoder on the FPGA has a number of instructions which are designed to poll the device or provide a procedure for interrupting certain processes such as data transfer and outputs. This is achieved by sending the instruction from the CPU to the decoder before it is performed by the FPGA. The idea is to make the command download and output the data file once it has been created. This means that the sound card is less complicated than the CPU to program as it only needs a number of commands to get it to work. The bulk of the program is written in the CPU. The below code identifies the process of waiting for the transfer to proceed.

Check register before data transfer

Wait

```
In A (StatusB)
Bit 5, A                //Test if ready
Jr Z Wait
Ld A (Sound byte)       //Output buzzer from card
Out A
Jr Ret                  //Jump back to program
```

This process is a little longer when the sound card needs to output a longer string of data contained in the memory. It first needs to download the audio file before it is output to the port.

Wait

```
In A (StatusB)
Bit 5, A                //Test if ready
Jr Z Wait
```

Transfer file

```
Ld B, File length
Ld HL, Start            //Load base address
```

```
Ld A, HL
Call Transfer          //Stores the audio file
RNC HL
Dec B                  //Loads the contents of the transfer
Jr NZ Next

Output file

In A (StatusB)
Bit 5, A               //Test if ready
Jr Z Wait
Ld A, 00001111         //Loads instruction to process file
OutB A,
Ret
```

This procedure describes transferring the file and outputting the file through the sound card. The FPGA can also be programmed to create an interrupt if a program needs access to the output port.

14.5.1 14.5.1 Interfacing the device and other peripherals

The device is connected to the CPU through the data bus as well as being connected to peripheral devices though a series of ports. The connection with the CPU to the FPGA is also shared by the VRAM memory which is used to store the data files. This can be seen in the diagram below which identifies the connection of the interfaces, along with the available connections that exist from the ports to any available peripheral devices.

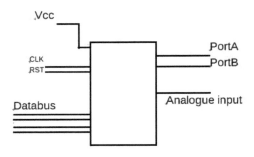

Fig 14.5.1 Interfacing the FPGA

As can be seen from the diagram the I/O interface allows an available connection to other peripherals. It also describes the connection for the transfer of data files.

End of Chapter Quiz

Design a CPU system?

What interfaces are used by the CPU?

Design a system with memory and without?

How is it possible to create a programme without a read only memory?

www.ingramcontent.com/pod-product-compliance
Lightning Source LLC
LaVergne TN
LVHW041205050326
832903LV00020B/464